CONTEMPORARY PSYCHOLOGY EXPERIMENTS:

ADAPTATIONS FOR LABORATORY
SECOND EDITION

CONTEMPORARY PSYCHOLOGY EXPERIMENTS:

Adaptations for Laboratory

SECOND EDITION

JOHN JUNG

California State University, Long Beach
Long Beach, California

JOAN H. BAILEY

San Jose State University
San Jose, California

JOHN WILEY & SONS

New York·Santa Barbara·London·Sydney·Toronto

Library of Congress Cataloging in Publication Data

Jung, John.
    Contemporary psychology experiments.

    Includes bibliographies.
    1. Psychology—Experiments—Laboratory manuals.
I. Bailey, Joan H., joint author. II. Title.
BR79.J86 1976   150'.28   76-7896
ISBN 0-471-45327-7

Library of Congress Catologing in Publication Data:

Printed in the United States of America
10 9 8 7 6 5 4 3 2 1

PREFACE

When *Contemporary Psychology Experiments: Adaptations for Laboratory* first appeared in 1966, there were few laboratory manuals available. Since then, a number of manuals have appeared, but we continue to find that our approach and philosophy is a distinctive and valuable means for teaching undergraduate experimental psychology.

We have retained 11 of the 15 original adaptations with little modification except an updating of the bibliographies and reference format. Seven new experiments have been added, which deal with more recent important topics ranging from sex-role bias to personal space and retrieval cues in memory. Experiments involving vital methodological problems such as experimenter bias, judgment biases, and evaluation apprehension also have been introduced.

As in the first edition, materials, procedural details, and suggestions for analysis of data are spelled out in detail, perhaps in too much detail to suit all users. We chose this approach so that the experiments could be used by beginning classes with little difficulty. For more advanced classes, we encourage the user to modify our adaptations to suit his needs and facilities.

A key feature of this new edition is the inclusion of supplementary or extension experiments for each of the 18 primary adaptations. Each extension provides background material on one or more problems related to the main experiment but does not include methodological and procedural details; this gives the class members or individual students a chance to plan these aspects of one or more related studies themselves. This strategy will prove instructive in allowing the student to discover some of the actual problems encountered and decisions that must be made in the planning and execution of experiments.

The extensions will allow the user a wider choice, since there will be, in effect, 36 rather than 18 experiments. More important, we hope that by doing at least two closely related studies, the student will gain a better understanding of the interrelationship of different studies from conception through execution to interpretation. Students will learn that one experiment often raises more questions than it answers, and that the results of one study are not only limited in generalizability to certain conditions but suggest other studies that should be done. Areas in which experiments yield results that contradict previous findings call for different approaches in the course of subsequent research than the areas where most results are in substantial agreement with established findings. In brief, it is hoped that in doing related studies the student will recognize some of the processes by which experiments and hypotheses are generated rather than limiting his learning to the technical aspects of conducting one isolated experiment.

The untimely death of Joan H. Bailey occurred just as this revision went into production. She was not only a valued colleague and treasured friend but also a dedicated teacher and wonderful human being who will be greatly missed.

Long Beach, California   **John Jung**

San Jose, California   **Joan H. Bailey**

To the Instructor

This collection of laboratory experiments was designed to offer the student an opportunity to gain experience in modern scientific psychology by providing a variety of new instructional contexts for both student and instructor. Laboratory workbooks for psychology have typically included experiments dealing with classical sensory, psychophysical, sensorimotor, and simple learning phenomena of psychology (e.g., the Müller-Lyer illusion), the method of limits, stylus mazes, pursuit rotor studies, and reaction time. These are basic areas of investigation in psychology and there is much merit in continuing their study, both in their own right and as methodological vehicles. However, contemporary psychology deals with many interesting phenomena which have not yet been incorporated in workbooks or manuals. In this workbook, we have adapted a selection of contemporary studies for instructional purposes.

One frequently hears the argument that the traditional studies should be utilized for laboratory instruction because clear-cut results are important for the beginning student, particularly in maintaining his interest. We consider this position debatable. In the first place, the phenomena of the classical experiments do not necessarily provide clear-cut results, as is evident with every new development in sensory psychology, signal detection, and so on. Moreover, we think a legitimate question can be raised as to whether it is realistic, or even honest, to lead the student to believe that all experiments arrive at definitive and easily reproducible results. Problems for which there are no easy and clear answers are frequently the ones that stimulate the student and induce him to learn.

The experiments in this workbook have been adapted from a wide sampling of research reports published in recent psychological literature. Appropriate references are cited for each experiment. By dealing with current topics in the research literature, the student is more readily introduced to original source materials since he is encouraged to compare his class results with those originally reported. Such a comparison frequently serves as a catalyst for deeper and more extensive examination by the student. These experiments have been "pretested" by the original authors and by the writers and have been found to yield analyzable results. However, there is a certain amount of risk—and excitement—as is always the case when one is dealing with relatively complex phenomena which may give rise to unexpected data.

Discussion questions following each experiment have been designed to encourage the student to consider modifications of our adaptations, to propose new questions for investigation, and to examine the possible effects of varying additional conditions.

Each adaptation has been designed as a true experiment in that it involves the manipulation of at least one independent variable and the examination of its effect on a dependent variable. Workbooks frequently contain exercises that serve only to demonstrate a given phenomena. It has been our aim not only to demonstrate phenomena, but also to allow the student to discover the effects of an experimentally manipulated variable. We have been particularly interested in developing adaptations of research on real and interesting psychological problems that can be carried out with only pencil, paper and the materials provided in this workbook. This feature has the additional virtue that all students in a class can perform the same experiment at the same time in a laboratory without elaborate equipment.

Introductory material has been provided as to the nature of the problems, procedures, phenomena, and expected outcomes of each experiment. We suggest that with this background information available, a useful procedure is to have the students serve as experimenters and obtain their own subjects from acquaintances outside the class rather than using each other as subjects for a substantial number of the experiments. We have found that this format encourages the student to become closely involved with the problems of actually conducting an experiment, from the formulation of the problem through the experimenter-subject inter- action, to the final analysis and interpretation of the data. The procedure of having each student run two or more subjects provides adequate data for analysis. It does require that data will often have to be collected by students outside of class, but the time required by this procedure is not excessive for any of the experiments and there are many lessons to be learned in the process. Moreover, the advantages that accrue from spending class sessions in discussing design and procedures, in combining data, and in discussing obtained data and interpretations of results more than offset any administrative problems that may arise from this procedure. A technique that we have found useful for combining data from all student experimenters is to provide a ruled ditto master on which each student records his data. The completed data sheet can then be reproduced in multiple copies, avoiding the necessity for each person to copy all the data.

All of the adaptations in this workbook have been designed so that they can be conducted and interpreted with the simplest of analytic procedures such as averages, percentages, and graphs. They can also be modified so that they may take the form of demonstrations. *For more advanced classes we have included suggestions for appropriate inferential statistical procedures so that more fully developed knowledge and skills can be applied.* Hence, this manual can be adapted to the beginning, the intermediate, or the advanced psychology student. It will probably find its greatest use in intermediate and advanced laboratory courses such as Experimental Psychology, Learning, and Motivation. However, it is also geared to a second course for psychology majors with or without a laboratory—the type of course usually designated as Advanced General Psychology, Principles of Psychology, Aspects of Psychology, etc. Moreover, a judicious selection from these experiments can provide enrichment for a beginning course in Introductory Psychology or General Psychology with an accompanying laboratory.

We are grateful to a number of people for their encouragement and suggestions during the developement of this workbook. In this connection we especially wish to thank Professor Carl P. Duncan and Professor James W. Sawrey. We are indebted to our students at California State College at Long Beach and at San Jose State College who found a number of flaws when we "pretested" these adaptations of contemporary experiments, but who bore with us nonetheless. We sincerely appreciate the efforts of Mr. William Emerson and Mrs. Phyllis Bermingham, graduate assistants of the junior author, for a careful and critical reading of an early version of the manuscript. We owe special thanks to our respective mentors, Professor Benton J. Underwood and Professor George E. Mount, for our original training in experimental psychology and for their encouragement, comments, and criticisms with respect to this workbook.

We also wish to express our appreciation to the authors of the experiments which we have adapted and the following publishers and journals who have granted us permission to paraphrase sections of certain articles, and to reproduce tables, stimulus materials, and brief excerpts:

American Journal of Psychology
American Psychological Association
Journal of Abnormal and Social Psychology
Journal of Experimental Psychology
Journal of Perceptual and Motor Skills
Journal of Personality
Journal of Verbal Learning and Verbal Behavior

J.J.
J.H.B.

To the Student

The experiments in this workbook provide you with a variety of adaptations of interesting experiments which are of current concern to psychologists. They cover a wide range of topics that have been shown to be amenable to experimental investigation, running the gamut from the determinants of the formation of impressions of the personalities of others to some of the factors influencing risk taking. Thus, you will be introduced to various problems and phenomena of interest in contemporary experimental psychology. Through these, you will also be introduced to certain methodological and procedural considerations which are common to experimentation in general.

This introduction to current research should prove to be a source of stimulation and interest for you, but a word of caution is also in order. Experiments seldom provide results which permit unequivocal "once and for all" answers. This is particularly true of some of the experiments included here since they deal with phenomena that are currently being explored. You cannot expect that your experiments will provide all the answers, or, in some cases, any answers. However, you can expect that your experiments and results should provide additional information and should raise further interesting questions. In short, you will have an opportunity to experience a taste of the fascination and challenge of psychological experimentation.

For some of the experiments in this manual, your instructor may require that you serve as the experimenter and obtain two or more experimental subjects. Your data will then be combined with those of your classmates. Variations in procedure from one experimenter to another could invalidate the entire experiment since there would be no clear basis for interpreting the combined class data. Hence, it is extremely important that you follow in detail all instructions given in the workbook and by your instructor. Make sure you understand thoroughly all points of procedure, i.e., the instructions you are to give to your subjects, the data you are to record, and how you are to summarize and present them for class compilation.

Ideally, the subjects selected for each experiment should either be obtained on the basis of some random selection procedure or should be matched on some relevant variable. In the latter case, subjects in different groups should be equated on some variable related to the dependent variable, for example, intelligence should be equated for different groups in a learning experiment. For our purposes, however, this will not usually be feasible. You can minimize this problem by attempting to select all of your subjects from the same range of age, intelligence, and background as agreed upon in class. The most convenient population will generally be college age students. In some cases, your instructor may be able to help you obtain subjects from introductory psychology classes.

Once you have obtained your subjects, it will be necessary for you to assign them to the two or more experimental and/or control conditions by some unbiased procedure. If there are only two subjects and two conditions, you can assign the first subject to one of the conditions by the flip of a coin, assigning the remaining subject to the second condition. If there are more than two conditions, you can assign a number to each subject and then assign the subjects to the several conditions by tossing a die, drawing numbers that have been well shuffled from a hat, using a table of random numbers, or some other deliberately nonsystematic procedure. (A table of random numbers is one that has been constructed with the use of some gambling device which gives each single digit an equal probability of occurrence.)

In experimenting with your subjects, it is important that you find a quiet room free from distraction and intrusion. You can avoid interruptions by placing a sign on the outside of the closed door reading "Experiment in progress. Do not disturb." Your attitude should be serious; however, you need not be strait-laced. You might begin the experimental session with a brief conversation to put your subject at ease since many subjects are highly anxious about any experiment or test. However, once the experiment begins you should refrain from any unnecessary comments, gestures, smiles, or frowns. Some studies, for example Rosenthal (1966), have shown that subtle unintended cues can often be misinterpreted by the subject and affect his performance on the experimental task. Be extremely careful in recording your data. If a mistake is made in recording, you should make an immediate correction. Similarly, exercise great care when presenting your data to the class and when copying results of the class. We have used the abbreviations S for subject M for mean, and SD for standard deviation on the data summary sheets at the end of each experiment.

Each of the experiments in the workbook includes detailed directions for procedures and suggestions for statistical analysis of your data and discussion of your results. Your instructor may have modifications or additional suggestions to propose. In addition, each student has the opportunity of examining new interpretations and proposing new questions that can be submitted to experimental examination.

In addition to each model experiment, a related study is briefly described in a supplementary or extension experiment. Details regarding experimental design and procedures are not provided for these "extension experiments" in order that you and your classmates can obtain first-hand acquaintance with some of the problems and questions that arise in the planning and conduct of psychological experiments. Furthermore, you will have an opportunity to see how studies are interrelated and often lead to still further experiments.

A formal report is customarily used to communicate the details of any research. Your instructor will probably require that you prepare such reports for some or all of the experiments that you conduct. These reports should include a statement of the background of the experimental problem, a description of the design and procedures used, an account of the obtained results, the statistical analyses of the data, and the author's interpretations of his results including their relation to the existing literature. The first section of the workbook describes some of the important considerations in writing such a formal report.

Last, but certainly not least, we wish to direct your attention and concern to your responsibility as an experimenter for the protection of the rights of your subjects. Your subjects are not only objects of scientific investigation but more importantly, they are also fellow humans, and are entitled to receive protection of their physical and psychological well-being during the experiments in which they serve. The ethical guidelines for psychological research are not easy to define in a few words; furthermore, there is no universal agreement among psychologists on some ethical issues as to what procedures are necessary.

The American Psychological Association created a committee to formulate a set of ethical principles for the conduct of research and their most recent recommendations have been published (American Psychological Association, 1973). Some of the varied reactions to this code can be found in the views of Baumrind (1971), Gergen (1973), and Resnick and Schwartz (1973). Other worthwhile discussions of ethical issues in research can be found elsewhere (e.g., Sasson & Nelson, 1969; Wolfensberger, 1967).

Some of the key aspects of the recommendations of the American Psychological Association principles (1973) are as follows. The experimenter should inform the participant about all features of the research that might reasonably be expected to affect his willingness to participate. If concealment or deception is required, the investigator should ensure the participant's understanding of the reasons for this action. The right of the individual to decline participation or discontinue further participation should be respected. Protection of participants from physical and mental discomfort, harm, and danger is also expected of the investigator and if such consequences may occur, the investigator must inform participants of this risk and attempt to minimize distress.

After the data are collected, the ethical investigator will inform the participant of the full nature of the study and clarify any misconceptions, especially those that might arise from deception. If the participation resulted in any undesirable consequences for the participant, there should be an attempt to detect, remove, and correct those consequences. Finally, it is to be indicated that the information obtained during the research is to be kept confidential.

It should be apparent that psychologists have given painstaking consideration to the ethics of research and we hope that you will do likewise. Finally, we should like to emphasize the necessity of adequate debriefing sessions after the participant has served. Not only is this an ethical responsibility so that the participant can learn what was done to him, but it also provides an opportunity for the investigator to see how the subject perceived the experimental task. The demand characteristics of an experimental situation, as Örne (1962) termed them, may be quite different for the participant from what the investigator intended so that incomprehensible results may occur. Talking with participants after the session can be very educational for the investigator, particularly with respect to discovering possible experimenter effects (Rosenthal, 1966). An amusing and biting cartoon by one of the senior author's students serves to illustrate this point most vividly and it is reproduced for your enjoyment and as a cautionary lesson. Our thanks to Colin Gray for his clever artistry and kind permission to reproduce his cartoon. Our thanks also to Karen Bennett and Janie Edwards, students of the second author, for their assistance in pretesting some of the new materials.

J. J.

J. H. B

REFERENCES

American Psychological Association, Committee on Ethical Standards in Psychological Research. *Ethical principles in the conduct of research with human participants*. Washington, D. C., 1973.

Baumrind, D. Principles of ethical conduct in the treatment of subjects: Reaction to the draft report of the Committee on Ethical Standards in Psychological Research. *American Psychologist*, 1971, *26*, 887–896.

Gergen, K. J. The codification of research ethics: Views of a doubting Thomas. *American Psychologist*, 1973, *28,* 907–912.

Orne, M. T. On the social psychology of the psychological experiment: With particular reference to demand characteristics and their implications. *American Psychologist*, 1962, *17,* 776–783.

Resnick, J. H., & Schwartz, T. Ethical standards as an independent variable in psychological research. *American Psychologist*, 1973, *28,* 134–139.

Rosenthal, R. *Experimenter effects in behavioral research*. New York: Appleton Century Croft, **1966.**

Sasson, R., & Nelson, T. M. The human experimental subject in context. *Canadian Psychologist*, 1969, *10,* 409–437.

Wolfensberger, W. Ethical issues in research with human subjects. *Science*, 1967, *155,* 47–51.

CONTENTS

CONTEMPORARY PSYCHOLOGY EXPERIMENTS:

ADAPTATIONS FOR LABORATORY
SECOND EDITION

In certain of the psychology courses the system of democratic blackmail is practised whereby you are forced to volunteer as experimental subjects or you lose 5% of your term mark.

However students, being the sophisticated devils they are these days, tend to spot the purpose of the experiment which can really foul-up the results sometimes. Hence the experimenters are forced to use elaborate red-herring, disguise techniques in order to further the ends of their 'science'.

In one experiment I was in, I figured it was concerned with group-cooperation. A team of five others and myself, with two buckets between us, had to transfer the water from the field house swimming pool to a series of polyethylene bags which were suspended from the ceiling of the old dining hall.

As we were panting up and down the hill, some guy in a white coat timed us with a stop watch and made sure we didn't spill any water. When all the water was safely in the old dining hall we had to complete a questionnaire to say how much we had enjoyed the experiment.

I discovered afterwards that the water-carrying bit had just been a subterfuge and that the questionnaire we completed was actually a test for latent homosexuality.

In the last experiment I had to take part in I found myself alone in a cubicle affair - just four bare walls. I figured the experiment was either about the general effects of sensory deprivation or possibly the isolation factor in stamina-destruction. Anyways, I stuck it out in there as long as I could but I finally collapsed after the fifth day.
It turned out that the actual experiment was next door but I had wandered into an empty broom-closet.

Reprinted with permission

1

GUIDE FOR WRITING EXPERIMENTAL REPORTS

The principal means of scientific communication is the research report. Over the years, the format of such reports has become standardized in a general way in all scientific fields. In psychology rather detailed standards have been set for journals published by the American Psychological Association (APA). These conventions are set forth in detail in the *Publication Manual of the American Psychological Association*. It is recommended that these guidelines be adopted in writing your own reports and be considered in evaluating reports that you read in the journals.

These conventions are concerned with the organization of the report and the style of presentation. Report writing should be both brief and *clear*. An examination of articles in the *Journal of Experimental Psychology* or the *Journal of Personality and Social Psychology*, which are available in your library, will give you a feeling for the style of writing that is most common.

When writing the report of an experiment, it is necessary that you include what is relevant to your problem. It is important that you indicate the theoretical basis or the prior observations which suggested the experiment. Furthermore, the report should make clear in reasonable detail the manner in which the experiment was carried out, that is, what was done to manipulate and measure variables in the manner demanded by the problem under investigation. This means that the report must be sufficiently detailed so that someone else could duplicate the experimental procedures. Finally, the report must state what results were obtained and what interpretation of these can be made.

The sections into which a report is conventionally divided are described below. Every report should contain all of the sections.

ABSTRACT

A brief (about 100 words) summary of the statement of the problem, procedure, results, and conclusions is to appear in this section. *Do not* include any new material that has not been covered elsewhere in the report. Also, this is *not* the place to introduce a moral or cliché statement. A brief and accurate summary of the full report allows the potential reader to determine quickly whether the study is relevant to his interests and, therefore, whether he wants to spend the time and effort to read it in full. As the body of literature grows with increasing acceleration, it becomes all the more important that abstracts accurately reflect the studies they purport to summarize, so that interested persons will not overlook important results because the abstracts did not properly reflect what was done in the research. Conversely, people do not like to get trapped into reading reports that prove to be useless to them because the abstract did not accurately convey the content of the experimental report.

Introduction

(*Note*: This section is not labeled.) This is a statement of what led up to the experiment and includes as much background material as is needed to place the experimental question in its proper setting. The problem may follow naturally as the next question from a body of previous research, it may simply have suggested itself as an interesting phenomenon, or it may follow as a deduction from a theory. It should be clear from the statements in the introduction what prior information is to be assumed in conducting the experiment and where the sources of this information are to be found. The experiment will necessarily deal with some matters that are speculative, and these should be indicated and stated in terms that can reasonably be supposed to be generally and reliably understood.

A common fault of students is the absence of a proper approach to the subject matter of the experimental report. You are (or should be) writing for everyone who might, at any time, be interested in the experiment and not for one or two people who presumably already know all about it. *You should not assume that your reader has any special knowledge of your experiment.* Since your report should be relatively "timeless," phrases such as "a few months ago" or "last week" should not be used. Do not include information based on personal experience which others cannot evaluate. Your personal reasons for conducting a particular experiment are not relevant. You may have been interested in the subject since you were a child, you may expect to get grant funds for research on this subject, or you may be doing it only because it is required for this course. Your reader is not concerned with your motivation. What he wishes to know is what contribution in terms of empirical knowledge, concepts, etc., the research offers him. You must explain or exhibit this information by relating your study to other pertinent work in the field of psychology, here and in the Discussion section.

METHOD

This section usually contains three parts, one describing the subjects, one describing the materials or apparatus employed in testing the hypothesis, and one describing the experimental procedure. It should be sufficiently detailed to permit duplication by any other competent investigator. Equipment items should be described in detail only when the information is needed to indicate what has been done in terms that will be reliably understood. Details of procedure, technique, or instrumentation that have been adequately described by earlier investigators should not be described in detail again, but references to the original sources should be cited.

The description of the procedure should summarize each step in the actual execution of the experiment, e.g., the instructions given to the subjects, the method of forming the experimental and control groups, and the order in which the various experimental and/or stimulus conditions were administered. The criteria here are the same as before. The description should be written in terms that you can reasonably suppose are generally and reliably understood and in sufficient detail to permit duplication by other qualified investigators.

Published research reports often assume that both reader and writer understand why certain aspects of the experimental procedure were conducted as they were. It is reasonable to assume that readers of technical articles have considerable background knowledge of the problems and methods in a given area. In this respect, it would be well for you to depart from the standard format and to indicate why you did what you did. Why were your particular procedures required by the questions to be answered, or in what way did they control some unwanted variable or variables?

RESULTS

This section should present a description of the data collected in the experiment and the analysis or analyses performed on them. It is desirable to summarize the results in tabular or graphic form in addition to the verbal description. A table or figure can frequently communicate your results far more effectively than words. Raw data should not be included in the Results section. Your instructor may ask you to include an appendix containing the raw data, computations, etc.

Graphs and tables should be concise and clear. They should be numbered and referred to by number in the text. A brief caption should be included describing the contents of the graph or table. The salient points brought out by each table or graph *must* also be stated in the text of the results section. The results of statistical analyses of the data are to be given in the body of the text and also in tabular form where tables will clarify the presentation. Such tables should indicate the number of subjects in each group, the mean value for each group or proportion performing in a particular fashion, and some measure of the variability of performance.

DISCUSSION

As indicated in the preceding section, a straightforward presentation of the results of the experiment is required. It is in this "Discussion" section that you should present your interpretation of the results obtained. You should give particular emphasis to any theoretical consequences of the results. You should also discuss any methodological considerations that you have found to be relevant. In considering the adequacy of the experiment as a test of the hypothesis, however, it does not suffice to show that a host of things was varying in an uncontrolled manner. You must specify how these uncontrolled variables could affect the results favorably or unfavorably. You should also indicate in your discussion the implications of this experiment for future research and for evaluation of relevant theories.

REFERENCES

When you refer to some existing work, you must always give proper acknowledgment by citing that work. See the *APA Publication Manual* or an APA journal such as the *American Psychologist* for the correct procedures for citing existing works.

There seems to be some misunderstanding concerning "references" and "bibliography" among students which we should clarify. References include those articles and other parts of the literature that are relevant to the problem which you refer to specifically. Any source that you have examined that you do not cite specifically cannot properly be included under your list of references but can be included, for purposes of student reports, under a separate list of sources labeled "Bibliography." As you will see from journal articles, published research reports include only references and do not have a bibliography section. However, students often read many sources which they do not cite, and they would like to mention them. These situations can be handled by citing such sources in a bibliography section which is distinct from the reference section.

REFERENCES

American Psychological Association. *Publication manual of the American Psychological Association* (2nd ed.). Washington, D. C., 1974.

1A
EXPERIMENT
EXPERIMENTER BIAS: THE EXPERIMENTER AS AN UNINTENDED FACTOR ON THE OUTCOME OF EXPERIMENTS

A number of investigators (Kintz, Delprato, Mattee, Persons, & Schappe, 1965; McGuigan, 1963; and Rosenthal, 1966) have pointed out the neglect of the influence of the experimenter's behavior and characteristics on results of studies. It is generally assumed that the experimenter runs the study in an unbiased manner. While this view may be generally valid in some areas (such as psychophysics or perception), there is a reasonable likelihood that aspects of the experimenter's appearance or behavior may modify outcomes of studies in social psychology, personality, and clinical psychology. These influences are unintentional and usually neither the subject nor the experimenter is aware that they are operating.

A good example of a variable that may affect results is the sex of the experimenter. Male and female experimenters may treat subjects differently; furthermore, subjects may react differently to experimenters of different sexes even if no bias emanates from the experimenters. Rosenthal (1967) referred to the former case as an active effect and to the latter example as a passive effect of the experimenter.

Harris and Masling (1970), for example, found that the sex of the experimenter influenced the production of responses to the Rorschach test. Male experimenters found differences in responding on this test between male and female subjects. Female experimenters, however, did not obtain these differences; thus it was concluded that some type of experimenter bias occurred.

Masling and Harris (1969) used a projective test, the Thematic Apperception Test (TAT), containing pictures to which subjects devised stories. They compared male versus female examiners when they administered TAT cards, some with sexual-romantic content. Male experimenters showed differential treatment of male and female subjects in that they presented these latter cards more often to females. Female experimenters apparently were more objective and did not show this type of bias.

7

The purpose of the present study is to examine the sex bias effect. However, since you are already fully aware of this potential source of experimenter bias, you cannot serve as experimenters for this study. Instead, you will conduct "an experiment within an experiment" in the fashion of the studies of Rosenthal (1966) on experimenter bias. You will recruit subjects who will act as your experimenters and they will test their own subjects. It is critical that you be as objective as possible in handling your experimenters so that you neither enhance nor reduce whatever tendencies they might have toward sex bias.

METHOD

Subjects

Obtain two subjects, one male and one female, from the same age range and background who will serve as your experimenters. Toss a coin to decide which sex to test first.

Materials

For convenience, a word association test will be used in this study instead of the Rorschach or the TAT. The following 10 words were taken from the Kent-Rosanoff (1910) word association list and will be used as the stimuli for the word association test: TABLE, DARK, MUSIC, SICKNESS, DEEP, SOFT, EATING, MOUNTAIN, HOUSE, BLACK.

Procedure.

Read the following instructions to each of your experimenters.

I need your help in conducting a study of word association. We need to test more subjects than I have time to test personally, so I want you to help me by testing four subjects, two male and two female. Locate four friends between the ages of 18 and 21 years. Test them in a mixed sequence with respect to sex, either MFFM or FMMF.

Here is a list of words that you will use for your tests. (Provide your experimenter with a copy of the list.) Give these instructions to your subjects:

I am going to give you a word association test. For each word I say aloud to you, I want you to write down as quickly as possible all the words that come to your mind which are related to the word I said. Tell me when you are ready and I will say the next word. You are again to write down all you associations. We will continue through a list of 10 words.

> There are no "right" or "wrong" responses; we just want to see how fluent you are in producing verbal responses to this list of words.

> Go through the list of 10 words at your subject's pace except that if your subject pauses for 15 seconds, interrupt and say "let's go on with the next word, ready?" Then say the next stimulus word.

After they have completed their data collection, explain to your experimenters the purpose of the experiment and the need for deceiving them.

Analysis of Data.

Determine the total number of associations given to the test list by each subject. Compute a 2 x 2 (sex of experimenter by sex of subject) analysis of variance. If any of the F values are significant, compare mean numbers of associations for appropriate experimenter-subject combinations using t tests for independent data.

DISCUSSION

1. Previous studies have shown a substantial difference between scores of male and female subjects tested by male experimenters, but little or no difference between male and female subjects tested by female experimenters. Did the results of your study agree with those findings?

2. Differences in behavior between male vs. female subjects, in themselves, do not tell us how much, if any, bias from the experimenter occurred. These differences may simply reflect genuine sex differences. However, if there is no experimenter bias and the difference of scores of male vs. female subjects is genuine, its magnitude should be equal for both male and female experimenters. Was it?

3. As indicated in questions 1 and 2, sex bias as a function of sex of the experimenter would be reflected in different magnitudes of differences between male and female subjects obtained by male and female experimenters. How would you explain the sex bias if it occurred?

4. Were there any genuine sex differences in your subjects' behavior, that is, differences not due to experimenter bias? If so, how would you explain the differences?

5. Do you think the type of words used as stimuli would make any difference in this study? Explain. You may want to examine frequency tallies for each stimulus word separately.

REFERENCES

Harris, S., & Masling, J. Examiner sex, subject sex, and Rorschach productivity, *Journal of Consulting and Clinical Psychology,* 1970, **34,** 60-63.

Kent, G. H., & Rosanoff, A. J. A study of association in insanity. *American Journal of Insanity,* 1910, **67,** 37-96, 317-390.

Kintz, B. L., Delprato, D. J., Mettee, D. R., Persons, C. E., & Schappe, R. H. The experimenter effect. *Psychological Bulletin,* 1965, **63,** 223-232.

McGuigan, F. J. The experimenter: A neglected stimulus object. *Psychological Bulletin,* 1963, **60,** 421-428.

Masling, J., & Harris, S. Sexual aspects of TAT administration. *Journal of Consulting and Clinical Psychology,* 1969, **33,** 166-169.

Rosenthal, R. *Experimenter effects in behavioral research.* New York: Appleton-Century-Crofts, 1966.

Rosenthal, R. Covert communication in the psychological experiment. *Psychological Bulletin,* 1967, **67,** 356-367.

SELECTED BIBLIOGRAPHY

Barber, T. X., & Silver, M. J. Fact, fiction, and the experimenter bias effect. *Psychological Bulletin Monograph,* 1968, **70,** 1-29. (a)

Barber, T. X., & Silver M. J. Pitfalls in data analysis and interpretation: A reply to Rosenthal. *Psychological Bulletin Monograph,* 1968, **70,** 48-62. (b)

Rosenthal, R. Experimenter expectancy and the reassuring nature of the null hypothesis decision procedure. *Psychological Bulletin Monograph,* 1968, **70,** 30-47.

1B
EXPERIMENT
INTERVIEWER BIAS: ON OUTCOMES OF INTERVIEWS

Not only can the results of experiments be affected by characteristics of the experimenter but it has also been found that similar biases can affect interviews (Berg, 1966; Hyman, Cobb, Feldman, Hart, & Stember, 1954). For example, Schatzman and Strauss (1955) found that social class differences between interviewer and interviewee are important determinants of interview behavior. Similarly, race differences between interviewer and interviewee are important. Kahn and Cannell (1957) recommended that minority group members be interviewed by interviewers of the same race to avoid bias. Indeed, Dohrenwend, Colombotos, and Dohrenwend (1968) have gone so far as to suggest that lower-class Black respondents will be biased in responses to White interviewers regardless of the attitudes toward Blacks that White interviewers may have. Sattler (1970) provided a summary of the studies on racial effects in interviews.

The investigation of interviewer bias is a worthwhile extension experiment to the experimenter-bias study. Age, sex, race, as well as psychological variables such as warmth, talkativeness, or hostility of the interviewer might well affect the responses of interviewees. Choose one variable and plan a study to investigate the effect of bias in interviews.

REFERENCES

Berg, I. A. The clinical interview and the case record. In I. A. Berg & L. A. Pennington (Eds.), *An introduction to clinical psychology*, New York: Ronald Press, 1966.

Dohrenwend, B. S., Colombotos, J., & Dohrenwend, B. P. Social distance and interviewer effects. *Public Opinion Quarterly,* 1968, **32**, 410-422.

Hyman, H. H., Cobb, W. J., Feldman, J. J., Hart, C. W., & Stember, C. H. *Interviewing in social research.* Chicago: University of Chicago Press, 1954.

Kahn, R. L., & Cannel, C. F. *The dynamics of interviewing*. New York: Wiley, 1957.

Sattler, J. M. Racial "experimenter effects" in experimentation, testing, interviewing, and psychotherapy. *Psychological Bulletin,* 1970, **73**, 137-160.

Schatzman, L., & Strauss, A. Social class and modes of communication. *American Journal of Sociology, 1955,* **60**, 329-338.

DATA SUMMARY ON EXPERIMENTER BIAS:
TOTAL NUMBER OF ASSOCIATIONS

	Male experimenter		Female experimenter	
	Male subject	Female subject	Male subject	Female subject
$S1$				
2				
3				
4				
5				
S_n				
	M SD	M SD	M SD	M SD

2A
EXPERIMENT
BIAS IN CLINICAL JUDGMENT:
ILLUSORY CORRELATIONS

Observation is susceptible to bias from a variety of sources. For example, if we have a favorable impression about someone, we tend to judge that person favorably in other situations as well, even if he does not deserve it. Stereotypes are another type of bias that may distort the accuracy of our subsequent observations. In situations where our past experiences and preconceptions mislead us into thinking that there are relationships between two variables when in fact there are none, we may speak of illusory correlations (Chapman & Chapman, 1967, 1971).

The situation in psychology in which a clinician makes diagnosis of clients observations of behavioral symptoms is one which is particularly likely to be biased by illusory correlations, according to Chapman and Chapman (1967). They hypothesized that projective tests, which are widely used by clinical psychologists, may be contaminated by these error tendencies. As an example, consider the Draw-A-Person test. The psychologist examines characteristics of the client's drawing of a person and attempts to infer something about his problem. One assumption that might be plausible is that someone who drew a picture with an unusually large head might be a person with anxiety and doubts about his intelligence. Yet, there is no available evidence to support such a hypothesis that has perhaps only metaphorical truth; that is, it sounds reasonable on the surface. Nonetheless, Chapman and Chapman found that experienced clinicians claimed that their observations supported views such as the one just described.
tions supported views such as the one just described.

In order to support their view that illusory correlations are prevalent with projective tests, Chapman and Chapman (1967) conducted a set of studies in which they presented subjects with alleged protocols from clients with differing diagnoses. Unknown to the subjects the alleged responses were presented equally, often in combination with each of the diagnostic categories, although in random order. Thus, there was in fact no real correlation between the responses and the diagnoses, but naive college students as well as experienced clinicians reported detecting certain responses more frequently in association with certain diagnoses.

Since such a relationship did not actually exist, these correlations were illusory.

As an explanation for this effect, Chapman and Chapman (1967) hypothesized that the observers probably had a strong preexisting association between certain diagnoses and certain expected responses. Thus, in the above example of the Draw-A-Person test, there may be a strong tendency for "intelligence" and "head" to be associated even before the drawings are presented. Support for this view is available in a verbal association study by Chapman (1967) in which he showed that even though words such as eggs, tiger, and notebook were paired equally often in combination with bacon over a series of trials, observers reported seeing eggs more frequently with bacon.

The purpose of the present study is to replicate Chapman and Chapman's (1967) concept of illusory correlation. Instead of using the materials from the Chapman and Chapman study, it is more convenient to use stimulus materials from Starr and Katkin's (1969) study in which they used an incomplete sentence blank rather than the Rorschach test. They paired five fictitious responses to different incomplete sentence stimuli with five hypothetical types of clinical cases. Even though no "symptom" occurred with any type of "diagnosis" any more than any other symptom, subjects did report illusory correlations since they claimed certain responses had occurred more frequently than others for each diagnosis.

In addition, Starr and Katkin (1969) compared the degree to which illusory correlations occurred among undergraduate students in clinical and nonclinical areas of psychology and graduate students in psychology. In our modification it would be interesting to make a similar comparison between psychology and nonpsychology undergraduates.

METHOD

Subjects

Obtain 2 male subjects and 2 female subjects. One member of each sex should be a psychology major and the other one a major in some other field.

Materials

In Table 2.1 are two copies of a table containing the 25 possible combinations of the five diagnoses and the five symptoms used by Starr and Katrin (1969). When cut out, a deck of stimuli containing 50 items is provided that should be thoroughly shuffled to produce a different random order for each subject.

Procedure

You may test both of your subjects together, provided you do not permit them to discuss their judgments with each other. Read the following instructions.

> We want you to participate in a task similar to that faced by a clinical psychologist so that we can test your powers of observation. One projective test used by clinicians is an incomplete sentence test in which the subject is given the opening of a sentence such as "I believe. . ." and his task is to complete it any way he sees fit, for example,". . . people are no good," or ". . . it is a nice day." We will show you a series of such responses that have been obtained from male clinical cases. Along with each sentence completion or "symptom," you will also be given a brief descriptive phrase identifying the main psychological problem of the man who produced that particular sentence completion. After you have had a chance to study all of the materials that I will present, I will ask you questions about what you remember. Since many cases have the same problem, do not be surprised if you see the same problem more than once. I will show you the pairs of sentence completions and problem description one at a time for about 10 sec each. Please pay attention as I can not go back or repeat any items. Any questions?

After you show the entire deck of 50 items to the subjects, give them the matching test in Table 2.2 with these instructions:

> On the left-hand side, you see five problem descriptions and on the right-hand side you see five different symptoms. I want you to try to recall what you just saw and indicate for each problem description which symptom or sentence completion occurred most frequently. If you think some of the sentence completions occured equally often for some types of problems, say so. (If you are testing two subjects together, do not let them discuss judgments.)

When the test is completed, ask your subjects what hypotheses or ideas they might have about the experiment. Postexperimental inquiry can frequently be of value in understanding the results. Then, explain the true purpose and reveal the deception that was involved. Try to justify the present study to the subjects in terms of the implications that illusory correlations have for many daily types of judgment.

Analysis of data

Combine the class data and determine how frequently each of the five sentence completion responses is selected as the one that occurred most often for each of the five problem descriptions. Since each response actually was paired equally often with each problem description, determine the extent to which the observers' judgments departed from chance expectancy. Compute a Cochran Q analysis for each problem description to determine whether the choices were randomly distributed among the five sentences from which the subjects had to choose. [See Hays (1963), chap. 18; Siegel (1956), chap. 7.] Make these comparisons separately for the psychology and nonpsychology student subjects.

If a substantial proportion of subjects reported a single sentence as the most common correlate of a particular description, you may wish to apply the binomial test to the difference between the obtained and chance (.20) probabilities. Your samples will probably be large enough that the normal approximation to the binomial test will be suitable for these comparisons (Hays, 1963, chap. 8; Siegel, 1956, chap. 4).

DISCUSSION

1. Assuming your results demonstrate illusory correlations, what were your subjects' reactions when you explained the actual frequencies of pairings?

2. Was there an equal tendency for illusory correlations to occur for all problem descriptions? If not, why do you think the effect was stronger where it was? Reflect on Chapman and Chapman's explanation for illusory correlations in general as a point of departure.

3. What variations in the test conditions might increase or decrease the magnitude of illusory correlations? Why?

4. Identify other situations besides clinical judgment in which illusory correlations might be prevalent. In education? Law? Popular opinions?

REFERENCES

Chapman, L. J. Illusory correlation in observational report. *Journal of Verbal Learning and Verbal Behavior,* 1967, **6**, 151-155.

Chapman, L. J., & Chapman, J. P. Genesis of popular but erroneous psychodiagnostic observations. *Journal of Abnormal Psychology,* 1967, **72**, 193-204.

Chapman, L. J., & Chapman, J. P. Illusory correlation as an obstacle to the use of valid psychodiagnostic signs. *Journal of Abnormal Psychology,* 1969, **74**, 271-280.

Chapman, L. J., & Chapman, J. P. Test results are what you think they are. *Psychology Today,* November 1971, pp. 18-22; 106-107.

Hays, W. L. *Statistics for psychologists.* New York: Holt, Rinehart, and Winston, 1963.

Siegel, S. *Nonparametric statistics for the behavioral sciences.* New York: McGraw-Hill, 1956.

Starr, B. J., & Katkin, E. S. The clinician as an aberrant actuary: Illusory correlation and the incomplete sentences blank. *Journal of Abnormal Psychology,* 1969, **74**, 670-675.

SELECTED BIBLIOGRAPHY

Golding, S. L., & Rorer, L. G. Illusory correlation and subjective judgment. *Journal of Abnormal Psychology,* 1972, **80**, 249-260.

Hammer, E. F. DAP: Back against the wall? *Journal of Consulting and Clinical Psychology,* 1969, **33**, 151-156.

Wanderer, Z. W. Validity of clinical judgments based on human figure drawings. *Journal of Consulting and Clinical Psychology,* 1969, **33**, 143-150.

TABLE 2.1: DIAGNOSIS–SYMPTOM COMBINATIONS[A]

P: Difficulty controling aggression	P: Difficulty controling aggression	P: Difficulty controling aggression	P: Difficulty controling aggression	P: Difficulty controling aggression
The happiest time—can never be	I regret—nothing I have done	At bedtime—I cry myself to sleep	The best—way to avoid trouble is to do nothing	My greatest fear—is too bad to talk about
P: Fears taking positive action	P: Fears taking positive action	P: Fears taking positive action	P: Fears taking positive action	P: Fears taking positive action
The happiest time—can never be	I regret—nothing I have done	At bedtime—I cry myself to sleep	The best—way to avoid trouble is to do nothing	My greatest fear—is too bad to talk about
P: Disturbed by sexual urges for other men	P: Disturbed by sexual urges for other men	P: Disturbed by sexual urges for other men	P: Disturbed by sexual urges for other men	P: Disturbed by sexual urges for other men
The happiest time—can never be	I regret—nothing I have done	At bedtime—I cry myself to sleep	The best—way to avoid trouble is to do nothing	My greatest fear—is too bad to talk about
P: Feels there is nothing to live for	P: Feels there is nothing to live for	P: Feels there is nothing to live for	P: Feels there is nothing to live for	P: Feels there is nothing to live for
The happiest time—can never be	I regret—nothing I have done	At bedtime—I cry myself to sleep	The best—way to avoid trouble is to do nothing	My greatest fear—is too bad to talk about
P: Perceptual fatigue and illness complaints	P: Perceptual fatigue and illness complaints	P: Perceptual fatigue and illness complaints	P: Perceptual fatigue and illness complaints	P: Perceptual fatigue and illness complaints
The happiest time—can never be	I regret—nothing I have done	At bedtime—I cry myself to sleep	The best—way to avoid trouble is to do nothing	The greatest fear—is too bad to talk about

[A] Adapted from Starr & Katkin, 1969.

TABLE 2.1: DIAGNOSIS—SYMPTOM COMBINATIONS[A]

P: Difficulty controlling aggression The happiest time—can never be	P: Difficulty controlling aggression I regret—nothing I have done	P: Difficulty controlling aggression At bedtime—I cry myself to sleep	P: Difficulty controlling aggression The best—way to avoid trouble is to do nothing	P: Difficulty controlling aggression My greatest fear—is too bad to talk about
P: Fears taking positive action The happiest time—can never be	P: Fears taking positive action I regret—nothing I have done	P: Fears taking positive action At bedtime—I cry myself to sleep	P: Fears taking positive action The best—way to avoid trouble is to do nothing	P: Fears taking positive action My greatest fear—is too bad to talk about
P: Disturbed by sexual urges for other men The happiest time—can never be	P: Disturbed by sexual urges for other men I regret—nothing I have done	P: Disturbed by sexual urges for other men At bedtime—I cry myself to sleep	P: Disturbed by sexual urges for other men The best—way to avoid trouble is to do nothing	P: Disturbed by sexual urges for other men My greatest fear—is too bad to talk about
P: Feels there is nothing to live for The happiest time—can never be	P: Feels there is nothing to live for I regret—nothing I have done	P: Feels there is nothing to live for At bedtime—I cry myself to sleep	P: Feels there is nothing to live for The best—way to avoid trouble is to do nothing	P: Feels there is nothing to live for My greatest fear—is too bad to talk about
P: Perceptual fatigue and illness complaints The happiest time—can never be	P: Perceptual fatigue and illness complaints I regret—nothing I have done	P: Perceptual fatigue and illness complaints At bedtime—I cry myself to sleep	P: Perceptual fatigue and illness complaints The best—way to avoid trouble is to do nothing	P: Perceptual fatigue and illness complaints The greatest fear—is too bad to talk about

[A] Adapted from Starr & Katkin, 1969.

TABLE 2.2: MATCHING TEST

Below are the five sentence stems and completions listed directly next to each of the five problem descriptions. For each of the descriptive problems, please choose the sentence completion that was most often associated with the problem description. Please indicate at least one choice for each problem description; a second choice may be noted if desired. If you feel that some of the sentences were associated equally frequently with a problem, please indicate this. Again, please do not discuss your judgments with anyone.

Problem	Sentence Completions
Difficulty controlling aggression	1. The happiest time—can never be 2. I regret—nothing I have done 3. At bedtime—I cry myself to sleep 4. The best—way to avoid trouble is to do nothing 5. My greatest fear—is too bad to talk about
Fears taking positive action	1. The happiest time—can never be 2. I regret—nothing I have done 3. At bedtime—I cry myself to sleep 4. The best—way to avoid trouble is to do nothing 5. My greatest fear—is too bad to talk about
Disturbed by sexual urges for other men	1. The happiest time—can never be 2. I regret—nothing I have done 3. At bedtime—I cry myself to sleep 4. The best—way to avoid trouble is to do nothing 5. My greatest fear—is too bad to talk about
Fears there is nothing to live for	1. the happiest time—can never be 2. I regret—nothing I have done 3. At bedtime—I cry myself to sleep 4. The best—way to avoid trouble is to do nothing 5. My greatest fear—is too bad to talk about
Perpetual fatigue and illness complaints	1. The happiest time—can never be 2. I regret—nothing I have done 3. At bedtime—I cry myself to sleep 4. The best—way to avoid trouble is to do nothing 5. My greatest fear—is too bad to talk about

A Adapted from Starr and Katkin, 1969

2B
EXPERIMENT
ILLUSORY CORRELATIONS IN "ORDINARY" JUDGMENTS

Chapman (1967) has reported illusory correlations in laboratory tests of judgments of ordinary words and the contexts in which they occurred. Pairs of words were shown to subjects such as BACON-TIGER. One of four different words always appeared on the left such as BOAT, LION, BACON, and BLOSSOM while one of three other words, TIGER, EGGS, and NOTEBOOK always appeared on the right-hand side of a stimulus pair. It was possible to create 12 different unique pairings of the left- and right-hand words.

A long series of trials (48-240 for different conditions) was given. In any series, all of the 12 possible pairings were shown equally often. Then a questionnaire was given asking the subject to judge the frequency with which each right-hand-side word had been shown in combination with each of the left-hand-side words.

Although the actual frequencies were 33 1/3 percent in all cases, Chapman predicted and found that word pairs that had high associative frequencies would be perceived as having occurred more often. BACON and EGGS, for example, like LION and TIGER were reported as having occurred together more frequently than they actually had. On the other hand, this was not true for pairs such as BLOSSOM-TIGER.

A worthwhile extension of Experiment 2A would be to replicate the occurrence of illusory correlations in a similar type of situation to show the generality of this judgmental bias.

REFERENCE

Chapman, L. J. Illusory correlation in observational report. *Journal of Verbal Learning and Verbal Behavior,* 1967, **6,** 151-155.

DATA SUMMARY ON ILLUSORY CORRELATIONS: NO. TIMES EACH STATEMENT JUDGED AS MOST FREQUENT FOR EACH PROBLEM

	Psychology Majors Statement						Nonpsychology Majors Statement				
Problem	1	2	3	4	5		1	2	3	4	5
1						1					
2						2					
3						3					
4						4					
5						5					

3A
EXPERIMENT
SEX ROLE BIAS AGAINST WOMEN BY MALE AND FEMALE SUBJECTS

Although there is currently much discussion and redefinition of sex roles in our society, it is true that much discrimination still exists against women. Whether stereotypes are the cause or merely the reflection of this bias is difficult to ascertain, but it is clear that males have traditionally been assumed to be dominant, independent, and active, among other things. On the other hand, females are depicted as dependent, passive, submissive, and gentle, to name a few traits (Rosenkrantz, Vogel, Bee, Broverman, & Broverman, 1968).

Not only have men generally regarded women as inferior in ability, initiative, and so on, but there is also evidence (Goldberg, 1968; McKee & Sheriffs, 1957; and Pheterson, Kiesler, & Goldberg, 1971) to suggest that women themselves tend to hold women in lower esteem. Self-deprecation has also been observed among other groups, such as ethnic minorities, which have been the target of discrimination (Clark & Clark, 1939).

It is difficult to be aware of many of our biases and many persons would deny that they are biased against women. For example, if a male professor assigns a low grade to a female student, is it partly due to his bias against women? Or is it because the paper is truly poor in quality? Under the circumstances, it would be difficult to demonstrate either case, but if we devised a situation in which the identical paper was graded under varying conditions, sometimes attributed to a male and sometimes to a female author, we would be able to examine the question. With this procedure, the paper quality is held constant and grades assigned to it under the two conditions should be equal if there is no sex bias.

Paradigms of this type have been used frequently in the study of prestige suggestion (Asch, 1948; Lorge, 1936; and Sherif, 1935) or as it is now termed, source effects (Hovland, Janis, & Kelley, 1952). In most of these studies, identical samples of written passages are differentially evaluated by subjects, depending on characteristics of the source to whom the material is attributed. For example, the same passage would probably get a higher rating if ascribed to a famous author than to an unknown author.

Goldberg (1968) employed a similar paradigm in his demonstration of sex bias in which he had subjects rate written passages on several dimensions of quality. For a given passage, half of the subjects were told it was written by a male while the other half was led to believe that it had a female author. Goldberg found sex bias in favor of male authorship; furthermore, this bias occurred not only for male raters but also for female raters.

A similar study (Fidell, 1970) has shown that judgments of brief professional profiles of hypothetical applicants for faculty positions in psychology departments are biased in the same fashion. When the same description of an applicant's qualifications was labeled with a male name, the hypothetical applicant was likely to be hired at a higher salary or academic rank if hired at all, than when it was associated with a female name.

A more extensive study by Mischel (1974) included male as well as female subjects who had to rate 700 word passages selected from professional writings in two male-oriented professions, city planning and law, and in two female-oriented professions, dietetics and primary education. Each topic was allegedly written by a male for half the subjects and by a female for the other half. Unlike Goldberg's (1968) findings, which suggested lower ratings by women for women authors regardless of the topic, Mischel found that ratings of the passages were higher for male authors only on the two topics where men would typically be regarded as more competent. Thus, sex bias against women may not occur in all areas or on all rating tasks. Mischel concluded that sex bias in these ratings may have reflected the subjects' use of knowledge about the true extent to which men and women are employed in various professions. Finally, it should be noted that the sex of the subject making the judgment did not appear to make any difference in the extent of sex bias in Mischel's study.

The present study will be patterned after Mischel's (1974) study, but no variation of the type of topic will be introduced. For each subject, half of the topics will be ascribed to male authors, while the other half will be attributed to female authors. A given passage will be associated with male and female authors equally often so that comparisons of the ratings of the same passage will provide an index of sex bias. In addition, use of both male and female subjects will allow determination of the extent to which sex bias is exhibited by males and females.

METHOD

Subjects

Each student should obtain at least four subjects, two male and two female, from the same age range. Toss a coin to determine whether they will be tested in a MFFM or a FMMF counter-balanced order, with respect to sex of subject.

Materials

Four passages of about 300 words each are presented in Tables 3.1 through 3.4. They are taken from introductory sections of various experiments in this lab manual, as you may recognize. An inspection of Tables 3.1 through 3.4 will show that each passage is reprinted twice, once with a male author and once with a female author.

Procedure

All subjects should read and judge the four different passages. Each subject should receive two passages with male authors and two other passages with female authors. Counterbalance the order of the articles so that the authors will be MFMF for one subject and FMFM for the other subject of a given sex. A summary of this procedure is provided below. Note that each passage is assigned male and female names equally often over your set of four subjects.

Passage	S 1	S 2	S 3	S 4
1	M	F	M	F
2	F	M	F	M
3	M	F	M	F
4	F	M	F	M

Read the following instructions to each subject:

We want to study writing quality of psychologists so we have selected four passages from journal articles. Please read each one at your own pace. Then I will ask you to rate each one immediately on the three dimensions of clarity, logic, and interest on this 7-point scale (give your subject a copy of the scale).

1	2	3	4	5	6	7
very poor	poor	mediocre	average	good	very good	excellent

After your subject reads each passage at his own rate, ask him to judge it immediately on each of the three dimensions—(clarity, logic, and interest) on the scale you have shown him.

After your subject has completed the final rating, explain the purpose, indicating the design of the study and the necessity for the deception regarding the authorship of the passages, and pledge your subject to secrecy until the study is completed.

Analysis of data

Calculate a single-factor with repeated measures (subjects by sex of author) analysis of variance based on the sum of the two ratings for the male author and the sum of the two ratings for the female author by each subject. Separate analyses will be needed for male and female judges (subjects) and for each dimension. (See Hays, 1963, chap. 13; Klugh, 1974, chap. 14; and Winer, 1971, chap. 4.) You can then compare the mean ratings for male vs. female authorship with t tests for dependent data, for example, for male subjects on a given dimension.

A more complex analysis, a two-factor design with repeated measures on one factor (sex of authorship) would permit sex of subject by sex of authorship comparisons (Klugh, 1974, chap. 14; Winer, 1971, chap. 7). Following this analysis, you could compare male vs. female authorship for male subjects and for female subjects; male vs. female subject differences for male authorship and for female authorship, and for any interaction between the two factors as appropriate. In undertaking such an analysis you should consider the question of whether it is proper to consider your sampling of subjects as leading to independent observations.

DISCUSSION

1. Did you find a bias against female authors? If so, was this tendency equally strong for both sexes?

2. Was sex bias present to the same extent on all dimensions? If not, can you account for its occurrence on the dimensions where it did occur?

3. Suppose you find that both male and female subjects included some high- and some low-biased individuals. What factors do you think might produce these individual differences? How could you test your views?

4.   Did there appear to be differences in intrinsic interest in the four passages irrespective of the alleged sex of author or order of presentation? If so, were the differences similar for male and female subjects? To examine these questions you may wish to use a 2 x 2 (sex of subject by sex of author) analysis of variance for each passage separately as Mischel (1974) did in her study. (See Klugh, 1974, chap. 13.).

5.   How might other variables such as age, socioeconomic status, or educational level affect degree of sex bias?

6.   How might the sex of the experimenter affect results?

REFERENCES

Asch, S. E. The doctrine of suggestion, prestige, and imitation in social psychology. *Psychological Review,* 1948, **55,** 250–277.

Clark, K. E., & Clark, M. P. The development of consciousness of self and the emergence of racial identification in Negro pre-school children. *Journal of Social Psychology,* 1939, **10,** 591–599.

Fidell, L. S. Empirical verification of sex discrimination in hiring practices in psychology. *American Psychologist,* 1970, **25,** 1094–1098.

Goldberg, P. Are women biased against women? *Trans-action,* 1968, **5,** 28-30.

Hays, W. B. *Statistics for psychologists,* New York: Holt, Rinehart, & Winston, 1963.

Hovland, C. I., Janis, I., & Kelley, H. H. *Communication and persuasion.* New Haven: Yale University Press, 1952.

Klugh, H. E. *Statistics: The essentials for research* (2nd ed.). New York: Wiley, 1974.

Lorge, I. Prestige, suggestion, and attitudes. *Journal of Social Psychology,* 1936, **7**, 386—402.

McKee, J. P., & Sheriffs, A. C. The differential evaluation of males and females. *Journal of Personality,* 1957, **25**, 356-371.

Mischel, H. N. Sex bias in the evaluation of professional achievements. *Journal of Educational Psychology,* 1974, **66**, 157—166.

Pheterson, G. I., Kiesler, S. B., & Goldberg, P. A. Evaluation of the performance of women as a function of their sex achievement and ·personal history. *Journal of Personality and Social Psychology,* 1971, **19**, 114—118.

Rosenkrantz, P., Vogel, S., Bee, M., Broverman, I., & Broverman, D. M. Sex-role stereotypes and self-concept in college students. *Journal of Consulting and Clinical Psychology,* 1968, **32**, 287—295.

Sherif, M. An experimental study of stereotypes. *Journal of Abnormal and Social Psychology,* 1935, **29**, 371—375.

Winer, B. J. *Statistical principles in experimental design* (2nd ed.). New York: McGraw-Hill, 1971.

SELECTED BIBLIOGRAPHY

Broverman, I. K., Vogel, S. R., Broverman, D. M., Clarkson, F. E., & Rosenkrantz, P. S. Sex-role stereotypes: A current appraisal. *Journal of Social Issues,* 1972, **28**(2), 59—78.

Fisher, L. E., & Kotses, H. Experimenter and subject sex effects in the skin conductance response. *Psychophysiology,* 1974, **11**, 191—196.

Goldberg, P. A., Gottesdiener, M., & Abramson, P. R. Another put-down of women? Perceived attractiveness as a function of support for the feminist movement. *Journal of Personality and Social Psychology,* 1975, **32**, 113—115.

TABLE 3.1
VERBAL CONDITIONING AND AWARENESS AS A FUNCTION OF INSTRUCTIONAL SET

WILLIAM F. CLARK, University of Oregon

In any interpersonal situation many subtle forms of verbal reinforcement may occur without any given person being aware of the process. That is, by some form of verbal approval, e.g., "good," "mm-hmmm," "yes," etc., it is conceivable that some aspect of the verbal behavior of a person is reinforced by the verbal behavior of another person in the situation.

Some experimental support for the existence of the phenomenon of verbal conditioning was found by Greenspoon (1955) who differentially reinforced singular and plural words. Subjects were instructed to say words as they came to mind. While they were responding, the experimenter murmured "mm-hmm" after all plural words for one group and after all singular words for a different group. A third group which did not receive this form of verbal reinforcement served as the control group. Greenspoon found evidence of verbal conditioning in the group reinforced for plural words but not in the group reinforced for singular words. Greenspoon's control group (no reinforcement) showed that singular words are emitted much more frequently than plural words. Hence, one explanation of the failure to influence the number of singular words by verbal reinforcement is simply that there is little room for an increase in this already strong tendency.

A more structured task was used by Taffel (1955). He presented verbs in the simple past tense typed one to a card in conjunction with the six personal pronouns. The task required subjects to compose sentences using each verb in conjunction with any one of the six pronouns. As in the Greenspoon study, subjects were not told the true reason for the study but were told that the experimenter was actually interested in some other purpose, e.g., to see how people make sentences. After a certain class of sentences (those starting with the arbitrarily chosen pronoun to be reinforced by the experimenter), some form of verbal reinforcement was

given. Evidence of verbal conditioning was shown when the proportion of sentences starting with the reinforced pronoun increased during the experiment while the proportion of those starting with nonreinforced pronouns did not.

TABLE 3.1
VERBAL CONDITIONING AND AWARENESS AS A FUNCTION OF INSTRUCTIONAL SET

JANET L. WILSON, University of Oregon

In any interpersonal situation many subtle forms of verbal reinforcement may occur without any given person being aware of the process. That is, by some form of verbal approval, e.g., "good," "mm-hmmm," "yes," etc., it is conceivable that some aspect of the verbal behavior of a person is reinforced by the verbal behavior of another person in the situation.

Some experimental support for the existence of the phenomenon of verbal conditioning was found by Greenspoon (1955) who differentially reinforced singular and plural words. Subjects were instructed to say words as they came to mind. While they were responding, the experimenter murmured "mm-hmm" after all plural words for one group and after all singular words for a different group. A third group which did not receive this form of verbal reinforcement served as the control group. Greenspoon found evidence of verbal conditioning in the group reinforced for plural words but not in the group reinforced for singular words. Greenspoon's control group (no reinforcement) showed that singular words are emitted much more frequently than plural words. Hence, one explanation of the failure to influence the number of singular words by verbal reinforcement is simply that there is little room for an increase in this already strong tendency.

A more structured task was used by Taffel (1955). He presented verbs in the simple past tense typed one to a card in conjunction with the six personal pronouns. The task required subjects to compose sentences using each verb in conjunction with any one of the six pronouns. As in the Greenspoon study, subjects were not told the true reason for the study but were told that the experimenter was actually interested in some other purpose, e.g., to see how people make sentences. After a certain class of sentences (those starting with the arbitrarily chosen pronoun to be reinforced by the experimenter), some form of verbal reinforcement was

given. Evidence of verbal conditioning was shown when the proportion of sentences starting with the reinforced pronoun increased during the experiment while the proportion of those starting with nonreinforced pronouns did not.

TABLE 3.2
IDENTIFICATION OF CONJUNCTIVE AND DISJUNCTIVE CONCEPTS

WILLIAM F. CLARK, Indiana University

A concept may be defined as a common attribute of several dissimilar stimuli which elicits the same response. "Table" is a concept which is applicable to a variety of stimulus objects which are commonly identified by their "tableness." Similarly "roundness," "largeness," etc., are concepts which refer to some attribute specifiable in a number of otherwise dissimilar stimuli.

Psychologists like Bruner, Goodnow, and Austin (1956) have been interested in studying how people form or identify concepts. A display of 81 stimulus cards which contained four different dimensions or attributes was used. Each card varied in (a) type of geometrical form (circle, square, or cross); (b) number of forms (1, 2, or 3); (c) number of borders (1, 2, or 3); and (d) color of forms and borders (green, red, or black). Thus there were three values of each of the four different attributes or stimulus dimensions which produced a deck of 81 different combinations, each instance exhibiting one value of each of the four attributes.

The general procedure in testing a subject was as follows: the subject was informed that the experimenter had a concept in mind and that certain cards in the display would illustrate it while others would not. First, he was shown a card which was a positive instance, i.e., it illustrated the concept that the experimenter had in mind. Then the subject selected cards in any order he chose from the display and the experimenter informed him after each choice whether it was a positive or negative instance. After each card selected by the subject, he could choose to offer only one hypothesis regarding the concept. This procedure continued until the subject correctly identified the concept. The use of paper and pencil was not allowed.

Bruner et al (1956) refer to a concept or a "category" of instances in terms of the defining attributes of some subset of the display. For example, the concept might be all cards with one red form or all cards with one form and/or with a circle. A distinction is made between conjunctive (C) and disjunctive (D) concepts. A conjunctive concept is defined by the *joint presence* of the appropriate value of two or more attributes, e.g., all cards containing red circles, i.e., redness and circleness occurring together. Disjunctive concepts are of an inclusive either/or [or both] nature, e.g., all cards that have red forms or have circles, or both.

TABLE 3.2
IDENTIFICATION OF CONJUNCTIVE AND DISJUNCTIVE CONCEPTS

JANET L. WILSON, Indiana University

A concept may be defined as a common attribute of several dissimilar stimuli which elicits the same response. "Table" is a concept which is applicable to a variety of stimulus objects which are commonly identified by their "tableness." Similarly "roundness," "largeness," etc., are concepts which refer to some attribute specifiable in a number of otherwise dissimilar stimuli.

Psychologists like Bruner, Goodnow, and Austin (1956) have been interested in studying how people form or identify concepts. A display of 81 stimulus cards which contained four different dimensions or attributes was used. Each card varied in (a) type of geometrical form (circle, square, or cross); (b) number of forms (1, 2, or 3); (c) number of borders (1, 2, or 3); and (d) color of forms and borders (green, red, or black). Thus there were three values of each of the four different attributes or stimulus dimensions which produced a deck of 81 different combinations, each instance exhibiting one value of each of the four attributes.

The general procedure in testing a subject was as follows: the subject was informed that the experimenter had a concept in mind and that certain cards in the display would illustrate it while others would not. First, he was shown a card which was a positive instance, i.e., it illustrated the concept that the experimenter had in mind. Then the subject selected cards in any order he chose from the display and the experimenter informed him after each choice whether it was a positive or negative instance. After each card selected by the subject, he could choose to offer only one hypothesis regarding the concept. This procedure continued until the subject correctly identified the concept. The use of paper and pencil was not allowed.

Bruner et al; (1956) refer to a concept or a "category" of instances in terms of the defining attributes of some subset of the display. For example, the concept mightt be all cards with one red form or all cards with one form and/or with a circle. A distinction is made between conjunctive (C) and disjunctive (D) concepts. A conjunctive concept is defined by the *joint presence* of the appropriate value of two or more attributes, e.g., all cards containing red circles, i.e., redness and circleness occurring together. Disjunctive concepts are of an inclusive either/or [or both] nature, e.g., all cards that have red forms or have circles, or both.

TABLE 3.3
RISK TAKING AS A FUNCTION
OF RANGE OF PAYOFFS

SUSAN J. EVANS, University of Texas

Whether or not we take risks or decide to gamble depends on numerous complex factors. Disregarding the totally reckless, most of us would probably ask ourselves the general question, is the risk worth taking? For example, suppose you are a healthy person and you are offered some vitamins of unproven quality. It is claimed that these pills will give you lots of pep, but it is possible that they may be injurious. The risk, in view of your current good health, is not worth taking. On the other hand suppose you are on your death-bed and some pills are offered which are guaranteed to restore you to an active life. Of course, they may also speed you on your way. Despite this unpleasant possibility, the risk here is more attractive. Thus, whether or not a person is willing to gamble, and hence win or lose, depends in large measure on his current state of health, wealth, or whatever he is risking.

Myers and Sadler (1960) devised a situation to study risk-taking behavior in which subjects could "win or lose" varying amounts of money on each of a series of trials. First, the subject was required to draw a card from a deck. A monetary outcome was printed on each card. This deck of cards contained 50 gains and 50 losses (+ and – values) of the same magnitude. An element of risk was introduced by then allowing the subject the choice of accepting the outcome from this deck on each trial or of gambling, that is, taking the risk that the outcome from a second deck might be more favorable. If the subject, after considering the Deck 1 outcome, elected to risk the Deck 2 outcome, he was obliged to accept the outcome of the second deck. Even if the subject chose not to gamble on a particular trial after viewing the Deck 1 outcome, he was always shown the Deck 2 outcome, the outcome he would have received had he decided to gamble. Trials consisting of fixed Deck 1 outcomes and the choice of whether or not to gamble on Deck 2 were continued until the two decks of 100 cards each were completed.

Myers and Sadler (1960) studied risk taking in this task as a function of the range of payoffs in Deck 2. The average payoff in the decks they used was zero but the range of payoffs varied. They found that when the Deck 1 outcome was a gain, the greater the Deck 2 range of payoff, the more the subject tended to gamble. On the other hand, large ranges of payoffs on Deck 2 led to less gambling on triais in which losses occurred in Deck 1.

TABLE 3.3
RISK TAKING AS A FUNCTION OF RANGE OF PAYOFFS

THOMAS P. RYAN, University of Texas

Whether or not we take risks or decide to gamble depends on numerous complex factors. Disregarding the totally reckless, most of us would probably ask ourselves the general question, is the risk worth taking? For example, suppose you are a healthy person and you are offered some vitamins of unproven quality. It is claimed that these pills will give you lots of pep, but it is possible that they may be injurious. The risk, in view of your current good health, is not worth taking. On the other hand suppose you are on your death-bed and some pills are offered which are guaranteed to restore you to an active life. Of course, they may also speed you on your way. Despite this unpleasant possibility, the risk here is more attractive. Thus, whether or not a person is willing to gamble, and hence win or lose, depends in large measure on his current state of health, wealth, or whatever he is risking.

Myers and Sadler (1960) devised a situation to study risk-taking behavior in which subjects could "win or lose" varying amounts of money on each of a series of trials. First, the subject was required to draw a card from a deck. A monetary outcome was printed on each card. This deck of cards contained 50 gains and 50 losses (+ and – values) of the same magnitude. An element of risk was introduced by then allowing the subject the choice of accepting the outcome from this deck on each trial or of gambling, that is, taking the risk that the outcome from a second deck might be more favorable. If the subject, after considering the Deck 1 outcome, elected to risk the Deck 2 outcome, he was obliged to accept the outcome of the second deck. Even if the subject chose not to gamble on a particular trial after viewing the Deck 1 outcome, he was always shown the Deck 2 outcome, the outcome he would have received had he decided to gamble. Trials consisting of fixed Deck 1 outcomes and the choice of whether or not to gamble on Deck 2 were continued until the two decks of 100 cards each were completed.

Myers and Sadler (1960) studied risk taking in this task as a function of the range of payoffs in Deck 2. The average payoff in the decks they used was zero but the range of payoffs varied. They found that when the Deck 1 outcome was a gain, the greater the Deck 2 range of payoff, the more the subject tended to gamble. On the othe;hand, large ranges of payoffs on Deck 2 led to less gambling on trials in which losses occurred in Deck 1.

TABLE 3.4
ORDER EFFECTS IN PERSONALITY IMPRESSION FORMATION

SUSAN J. EVANS, University of Massachusetts

How do we form our impressions about the personalities of people we meet? Personality refers to a combination of traits inferred from samples of observed behavior of the person in question. Although the observations we make of a person on our initial encounter do not permit an accurate or complete determination of his personality, nonetheless it is evident that we are continually forming impressions of personality on the basis of limited contact with other people, regardless of the accuracy of such judgments.

There may be considerable truth to the adage "first impressions are lasting ones." In any case, we do tend to classify and judge personality from limited initial impressions. Some experimental evidence to support this assertion comes from Asch (1946). He had subjects report impressions of a hypothetical person who was described by the experimenter using a list of adjectives allegedly applicable to the fictitious person to be judged. This list included both favorable and unfavorable adjectives applicable to the fictitious person; however, the order in which the list of adjectives was presented differed for the two groups. In one group the favorable adjectives were read first, followed by the unfavorable ones, whereas in the other group the opposite order was used.

Asch found that the impressions formed were related to the type of adjectives read first, i.e., the same list evoked favorable impressions in the group receiving favorable adjectives first, whereas it evoked unfavorable impressions in the group receiving unfavorable adjectives first. Apparently, then, *primacy* is an important factor in impression formation.

Such primacy effects in impression formation from a list of adjectives have also been found by Anderson (1965). However, there is less agreement regarding the underlying causes for such primacy effects. Asch hypothesized that the meanings of later adjectives on the list are actually modified by the context set up by the initial adjectives presented

to the subject. Thus, if favorable adjectives are received first, they make the following unfavorable words seem less unfavorable. On the other hand, if unfavorable adjectives are presented first, they affect the subsequent favorable adjectives adversely with the result that they appear less favorable.

TABLE 3.4
ORDER EFFECTS IN PERSONALITY IMPRESSION FORMATION

THOMAS P. RYAN, University of Massachusetts

How do we form our impressions about the personalities of people we meet? Personality refers to a combination of traits inferred from samples of observed behavior of the person in question. Although the observations we make of a person on our initial encounter do not permit an accurate or complete determination of his personality, nonetheless it is evident that we are continually forming impressions of personality on the basis of limited contact with other people, regardless of the accuracy of such judgments.

There may be considerable truth to the adage "first impressions are lasting ones." In any case, we do tend to classify and judge personality from limited initial impressions. Some experimental evidence to support this assertion comes from Asch (1946). He had subjects report impressions of a hypothetical person who was described by the experimenter using a list of adjectives allegedly applicable to the fictitious person to be judged. This list included both favorable and unfavorable adjectives applicable to the fictitious person; however, the order in which the list of adjectives was presented differed for the two groups. In one group the favorable adjectives were read first, followed by the unfavorable ones, whereas in the other group the opposite order was used.

Asch found that the impressions formed were related to the type of adjectives read first, i.e., the same list evoked favorable impressions in the group receiving favorable adjectives first, whereas it evoked unfavorable impressions in the group receiving unfavorable adjectives first. Apparently, then, *primacy* is an important factor in inpression formation.

Such primacy effects in impression formation from a list of adjectives have also been found by Anderson (1965). However, there is less agreement regarding the underlying causes for such primacy effects. Asch hypothesized that the meanings of later adjectives on the list are actually modified by the context set up by the initial adjectives presented

to the subject. Thus, if favorable adjectives are received first, they make the following unfavorable words seem less unfavorable. On the other hand, if unfavorable adjectives are presented first, they affect the subsequent favorable adjectives adversely with the result that they appear less favorable.

3B
EXPERIMENT
SEX ROLE STEREOTYPES AND JUDGMENTS OF MENTAL HEALTH

There is evidence that clinical psychologists hold stereotypes of women that contain attributes generally held to be characteristic of persons who are not mentally healthy. Broverman, Broverman, Clarkson, Rosenkrantz, and Vogel (1970) asked a sample of professional clinicians to answer a questionnaire containing 122 bipolar trait items, such as *very subjective* to *very objective*. Instructions called for checking off the traits that the clinicians felt characterized an adult who was mentally healthy. In addition, they were asked to depict the healthy male and the healthy female. Results showed a high correlation between the stereotypes of healthy adult and healthy male, whereas the concept of healthy female differed substantially from both the concepts of healthy adult and healthy male. Women were characterized by such traits as *more submissive, less independent, less aggressive, more emotional,* and *less objective*, to name a few. These traits were regarded as more typical of persons lacking in mental health. It should be noted that female as well as male clinicians made these judgments.

What is the layman's stereotype of a mentally healthy person? Does the layman's conception of a mentally healthy male match this profile more closely than the conception of a mentally healthy female? An interesting extension of the Broverman et al. (1970) study might be to assess these stereotypes with subjects taken from the general population. Or, in view of recent increases in awareness of this issue, perhaps a comparison of persons who are pro- vs. con-Women's Lib might disclose interesting differences either in mentally healthy stereotypes or in scores on the Attitude Toward Women Scale (Spence & Helmreich, 1972).

REFERENCES

Broverman, I. K., Broverman, D. M., Clarkson, F. E., Rosenkrantz, P. S., & Vogel, S. R. Sex role stereotypes and clinical judgments of mental health. *Journal of Consulting and Clinical Psychology,* 1970, **34**, 1–7.

Spence, J. T., & Helmreich, R. The Attitudes Toward Women Scale: An objective instrument to measure attitudes toward the rights and roles of women in contemporary society. *J S A S Catalogue of Selected Documents in Psychology,* 1972, **2,** 66. (Ms. No. 153)

DATA SUMMARY ON SEX ROLE STEREOTYPES: RATINGS OF PASSAGES

	Male Subjects							Female Subjects					
	Author							Author					
	Male			Female				Male			Female		
Dimension [a]	1	2	3	1	2	3		1	2	3	1	2	3
$S1$													
2													
3													
4													
5													
S_n													

[a] Dimensions
1 Clarity
2 Logic
3 Interest

4A
EXPERIMENT
CONTEXT EFFECTS IN JUDGMENTS
OF LENGTHS OF LINES

According to Helson (1959, 1964) all behavior is affected by three broad classes of stimuli. These three classes are (a) the stimuli being immediately attended to; (b) all other stimuli present at the time which serve as a context for the first type of stimuli, and (c) all other determinants of behavior such as past experience and organismic factors, which interact with the current stimulation. The pooled effect of these three classes of stimuli constitutes what Helson calls the "adaptation level" for the organism which it uses as a reference point for making discriminations and judgments concerning its immediate environment. According to Helson's proposal, the adaptation level (AL) defines the basis for the reaction of the organism to its present conditions of stimulation.

Phenomena in problem areas ranging from psychophysics and perception, on the one hand, to personality and social behavior on the other can be considered to involve common principles if they are viewed as representing behavioral adaptations of the organism to external and internal factors.

According to Helson, when stimuli are assigned to categories along a continuum by a number of subjects, the category scale derived from these psychophysical judgments is centered at the mean of all relevant stimuli of these three classes. (For an advanced discussion of scaling, see Guilford. 1954.)

On the other hand, Parducci (1963, 1965) and his colleagues (e.g., Parducci, Calfee, Marshall, & Davidson, 1960) have obtained results that are incompatible with Helson's formulation. They have compared the influence of different stimulus contexts on perceptual judgment and, contrary to Helson's theory, variation in the means of the stimulus contexts do not affect judgment, whereas differences in either the midpoints or the medians of the stimulus distributions do.

On the basis of these findings, Parducci (1963, 1965) proposed a range-frequency compromise hypothesis that is clearly and briefly presented in nontechnical terms elsewhere (Parducci, 1968). Briefly, it is maintained that two principles are used in making judgments, a range principle such that the subject tries to use as many subsets as he has category labels to use, and a frequency principle such that the subject tries to assign equal numbers of stimuli to each of the categories. Use of the first principle should make the midpoint of the distribution an index of adaptation level, whereas the use of the second principle would make the median represent the central tendency of judgment. In actuality, both rules are applied so that the value of the adaptation level is a compromise that falls between the value of the median and the midpoint of the stimulus set. Contrary to Helson, the mean of the set is irrelevant.

Parducci tested his theory by comparing judgments with contexts where only one measure of central tendency was varied and the other two indices were held constant. His results, as reported above, showed that only variations in either median or midpoint made any differences on the judgments, thus confirming his formulation.

The present study is concerned with the effects of different contexts on simple perceptual judgments. It is based on a study by Parducci and Marshall (1961) in which subjects were required to make judgments of lengths of lines which were presented in sets differing distributions of lengths. Each subject was to assign a numerical label to each line ranging from 1 (very short) to 6 (very long), thus assigning each line to one of six categories. The distributions of lines differed in the values of the arithmetic means, medians, or midpoints to permit determination of how these parameters affected the scale of judgment. These parameters were different from Helson's proposed geometric mean.

Parducci and Marshall (1961) found that the variation in arithmetic means of the set of lines was not an effective variable. Only the variation in midpoints (the mean of the two extreme lengths of a set) and medians had significant effects on the centering of the scale of judgment (adaptation level with respect to the category scale).

This experiment replicates the essential features of the Parducci and Marshall (1961) experiment and permits comparison of the effects of two values of the arithmetic means, two values of the medians, and two values of the midpoints in the distributions of line lengths.

METHOD

Subjects

Each E should obtain six subjects, one for each condition, that is, for the six different distributions of line lengths. Devise some unbiased method of assigning subjects to the six conditions.

Materials

Six different sets of 45 lines which differ in the distribution line lengths will be used. (See Tables 4.2 through 4.7 for stimulus sets A through F at the end of this experiment.) For each set, the 45 successive lines are ordered with respect to length with the longest line at the top of the page and printed parallel to the short side of the page. Table 4.1 shows the distributions of the lengths of the lines in the six sets. The differences in the lengths of successive lines for a given set are approximately equal for each set of the 20-millimeter intervals shown in Table 4.1.

It should be noted that while the mean value varies in the high and low mean conditions, the midpoints and medians are constant at 100 millimeters, the medians are varied between the high and low median conditions while the means and midpoints are held constant at 100 millimeters, and the midpoints are varied between high and low midpoint conditions, while the means and medians are held constant at 100 millimeters.

Procedure

After seating the subject in a quiet room, read the following instructions to him:

On this sheet that I will give you is a set of lines in order of decreasing length. Keep the sheet before you so that the lines are placed horizontally. You are to examine the entire set and then judge how long or short each line is relative to all the other lines. Use the following categories to make your judgments and record to

Table 4.1: Number of Lines in Each 20-Millimeter Interval of Length (Adapted from Parducci & Marshall, 1961)

	Stimulus Set	10-29	30-49	50-69	70-89	90-109	110-129	130-149	150-169	170-189
A	High Mean	3	3	3	11	5	3	3	3	11
B	Low Mean	11	3	3	3	5	11	3	3	3
C	High Median	6	2	2	2	10	17	2	2	2
D	Low Median	2	2	2	17	10	2	2	2	6
E	High Midpoint	0	0	12	6	9	12	2	2	2
F	Low Midpoint	2	2	2	12	9	6	12	0	0

the right of each line the number that reflects your judgment of the length category into which each line falls.

6 very long
5 long
4 slightly longer than average
3 slightly shorter than average
2 short
1 very short

Start at the top of the page and do not skip any lines. Take your time and make careful judgments, but don't try to devise special rules for judging. The purpose of this experiment is to learn how people in general compare the lengths of different lines.

Allow your subjects about 10 minutes to complete the task.

Analysis of data

Determine the actual lengths in millimeters of the longest line judged "3" and the shortest line judged "4" for each of your six subjects. The arithmetic average of these two lengths determines the adaptation level (AL), as determined by Parducci and Marshall for each subject. Combine these values for your six subjects with those of the rest of the class for the respective conditions. Compute the mean and standard deviation for the combined results for each of the six experimental conditions and place them in tabular form. Be sure to label your table appropriately.

Compute a 3 x 2 (parameter by level) analysis of variance to determine overall effects. Then compute t tests for uncorrelated data between the high and low mean (A and B), median (C and D), and midpoint (E and F) conditions.

DISCUSSION

1. How do your class results compare with those of Parducci and Marshall (1961) with respect to: (a) the mean contexts; (b) the median contexts; (c) the midpoint contexts?

2. If your class data are in disagreement with those of Parducci and Marshall, what factors might be responsible? Do your data support different conclusions?

3. Suggest other ways in which the effects of context on length judgment could be studied.

4. Suggest other types of judgments or situations where context effects might be important and could be studied. Can you suggest ways in which they might be studied?

5. Do you think that certain types of experiences lead to more resistance to the influences of context on judgment? Give examples.

REFERENCES

Guilford, J. P. *Psychometric methods.* New York: McGraw-Hill, 1954.

Helson, H. Adaptation level theory. In S. Koch (Ed.), *Psychology: A study of science* (Vol. 1). New York: McGraw-Hill, 1959.

Helson, H. *Adaptation-level theory: An experimental and systematic approach to behavior.* New York: Harper & Row, 1964.

Parducci, A. Range-frequency compromise in judgment. *Psychological Monographs,* 1963, **77,** (2, Whole No. 565).

Parducci, A. Category judgment: A range-frequency model. *Psychological Review,* 1965, **72,** 407–418.

Parducci, A. The relativism of absolute judgments. *Scientific American,* 1968, **219,** 84–93.

Parducci, A., & Marshall, L. M. Context effects in judgments of length. *American Journal of Psychology,* 1961, **74,** 576–583.

Parducci, A., Calfee, R. C., Marshall, L. M., & Davidson, L. P. Context effects in judgment: Adaptation level as a function of the mean, midpoint, and median of the stimuli. *Journal of Experimental Psychology,* 1960, **60,** 65–77.

SELECTED BIBLIOGRAPHY

Nunnally, J. C. *Psychometric theory.* New York: McGraw-Hill, 1967.

Parducci, A. An adaptation level analysis of ordinal effects in judgment. *Journal of Experimental Psychology,* 1959, 58, 239–2466.

DATA SUMMARY ON CONTEXT EFFECTS IN JUDGMENTS OF LENGTHS OF LINES (ARITHMETIC AVERAGE IN MILLIMETERS OF LINES JUDGED "3" AND LINES JUDGED "4")

Context	Mean		Median		Midpoint	
	High	Low	High	Low	High	Low
S 1						
2						
3						
4						
5						
S_n	M SD	M SD	M SD	M SD	M SD	M SD

Table 4.2: Stimulus Set A

Table 4.3: Stimulus Set B

Table 4.4: Stimulus Set C

Table 4.5: Stimulus Set D

Table 4.6: Stimulus Set E

Table 4.7: Stimulus Set F

4B
EXPERIMENT
SHIFTS IN JUDGMENTS AS
EFFECTS OF ANCHORING STIMULI

One interesting aspect of the influence of context effects that has been investigated is that of shifts in judgments as a function of anchoring stimuli added to the regular stimulus series. In anchoring studies, stimulus values that are within or beyond the limits of the regular stimuli are introduced to determine their effects on the later judgments of the regular stimulus series. In effect, these situations represent context effects across successive tasks as opposed to a single judgmental task, but they deal with the same basic processes of establishing and modifying scales of judgment and reflect the relativity of judgments.

A commonly observed anchoring effect is that of contrast in which the mean judgments of the standard stimulus series shift between the last presentation prior to the introduction of the anchor stimuli and the anchor or the first post-anchor presentations. The shift is downward for high anchor stimuli and upward for low anchor stimuli. A less consistent effect observed in some studies of anchoring is that of assimilation in which post-anchor presentations of the standard stimuli result in judgments that return toward and sometimes overshoot the pre-anchor presentation judgments.

Anchoring of psychophysical judgments has also been of interest because of analogies to certain phenomena of social and clinical judgments (Bieri, Atkins, Briar, Leaman, Miller, & Tripodi, 1966). For example, an extreme political position may be judged as "moderate" after the person is exposed to an even more extreme position. On the other hand, a very prejudiced person exposed to anti-prejudice propaganda may return to an even stronger adherence to his original position, the so-called "boomerang effect" (Sherif, Taub, & Hovland, 1958, p. 150).

Parducci, Perrett, and Marsh (1969) investigated anchoring stimuli in a before-after design in order to examine their effects in the framework of the range-frequency theory of judgment (Parducci, 1965). Parducci et al. (1969) employed a set of nine dark squares with side lengths ranging in progressive steps from 5.4 centimeters (.054 meters) to 23.2 centimeters (.232 meters). Five intermediate-sized squares, stimuli 3-7, were presented to all subjects for size judgments in the pre-anchoring conditions. Three separate anchoring groups followed using: (a) five large squares, stimuli 5-9, for the high-anchor condition; (b) five small squares, stimuli 1-5, for the low-anchor condition, and (c) the same five intermediate squares, stimuli 3-7, for the control condition. All three groups received the original five intermediate-sized squares, stimuli 3-7, in the post-anchoring judgments.

In addition, Parducci et al. (1969) used four different instructions ranging from a fixed set of verbal categories through numerical identifications similar to magnitude estimations in order to structure the scaling task for different kinds of judgmental language. They found the customary contrast effect, that is, shifts away from the values assigned to the anchors, in all four instruction conditions. Following removal of the anchors, judgments gradually shifted back toward the pre-anchor levels. One surprising result was that in the condition where numerical identifications were used, the contrast effect gave way to an assimilation effect in the post-anchor trials.

An interesting extension of Experiment 4A would be to replicate certain instruction conditions of the Parducci et al. (1969) experiment, particularly those leading to possible assimilation and contrast effects of anchoring stimuli. You might wish to expand your investigation to examine the effects of near and distant anchors.

REFERENCES

Bieri, J., Atkins, A., Briar, S., Leaman, R. L., Miller, H., & Tripodi, T. *Clinical and social judgment.* New York: Wiley, 1966.

Parducci, A. Category judgment: A range-frequency model. *Psychological Review,* 1965, **72,** 407–418.

Parducci, A., Perrett, D. S., & Marsh, H. W. Assimilation and contrast as range-frequency effects of anchors. *Journal of Experimental Psychology,* 1969, **81,** 281–288.

Sherif, M., Taub, D., & Hovland, C. I. Assimilation and contrast effects of anchoring stimuli on judgments. *Journal of Experimental Psychology,* 1958, **55,** 150–155.

5A
EXPERIMENT
BINARY PREDICTION AS A FUNCTION
OF REINFORCEMENT SCHEDULE

In recent years there has been considerable interest in the study of human prediction behavior in a rather simple situation known as the *binary choice experiment*. In this type of experiment the subject is asked to predict which of two (and only two) possible alternative events will occur on each trial of a series of trials. After the subject makes his prediction he is shown or told which event actually occurs. The occurrence of each event and the frequency with which each of the two events occurs are determined by the experimenter. The particular sequence of events which is known as the reinforcement schedule is usually predetermined by the experimenter, using some method of randomization. Thus each event in the sequence occurs independently of the sequence of events that has already occurred, and independently of the predictions of the subject. The subject, of course, is unaware that the sequence of events is a predetermined random sequence. He is instructed to make as many correct predictions as possible in order to study how he will attempt to do this.

According to probability theory, the number of correct predictions of events in a random sequence can be maximized only if the subject predicts the most frequent alternative on *every* trial. However, subjects tend to divide their responses between the two alternatives in such a way that they predict the two events in about the same proportions that they actually occur in the sequence. This phenomenon, known as "probability matching," seems to be a very stable strategy or behavior on the part of the subjects in this kind of situation.

The results of an experiment by Estes and Straughan (1954) illustrate probability matching. The subject was placed in front of two telegraph keys. If he pressed the correct key on a given trial, he was so informed by a light which went on above that key. Of course, the schedule of correct outcomes had been predetermined by the experimenter through a process of random assignment. Three groups of subjects were run for 240 consecutive trials. During the first 120 trials, the groups differed in the reinforcement schedules of the two alternatives, i.e., 30-70, 50-50, and 85-15. On the last 120 trials all three groups received 30-70 reinforcement schedules of the two alternatives. In all cases, probability matching behavior was quite striking, especially during the later trials.

This experiment replicates portions of the Estes and Straughan (1954) study. A comparison will be made of the effects of two different reinforcement schedules on binary choice predictions.

METHOD

Subjects

Each experimenter will obtain two subjects, one for each reinforcement schedule condition. Flip a coin to determine which of the two reinforcement schedules will be used for your first subject. Use the remaining schedule for your second subject.

Materials

Prepare two stimulus figures, one a circle and the other a square, on 3 x 5 cards to serve as the two events or alternatives. Two random sequences of events differing in the relative proportions of the two alternatives will determine the order of presentation of the two stimuli over 100 trials. Schedule A (see Data Summary at the end of this experiment) will reinforce one alternative 80% of the time and the other alternative 20% of the time (80-20). Schedule B (see Data Summary) will reinforce one alternative 60% of the time and the other alternative 40% of the time (60-40). Half of the experimenters will reinforce the circle most frequently and half of the experimenters will reinforce the square most frequently. Assign experimenters to circle and square conditions in counterbalanced order (ABBA).

One method of generating these sequences provides that the designated proportions of the two outcomes will occur within each block of 10 trials, and that within each block of 10 trials, the outcomes will occur in a nonsystematic order. To generate Schedule A, find 10 similar objects, eight of one color and two of another color, e.g., checkers. One color will represent one stimulus and the other color will represent the other stimulus. Place all of these objects in a container and be sure that they are well mixed. Then remove objects one at a time, recording the outcome that each object represents as you take it from the container. This will give you the first 10 outcomes in the total sequence. Repeat this procedure 10 times, always being sure that the objects are well mixed in the container. Schedule B can be generated in the same way, using six and four objects respectively.

Procedure

After seating your subject in a place free from distraction, read the following instructions:

> The purpose of this experiment is to study how people make predictions in a simple two-choice situation. I will show you a series of figures, each of which will be either a circle or a square. Before I present each figure, I will give you a ready signal—the word "now." When you hear "now," you are to predict which figure you expect will be presented. After I have recorded your prediction, I will show you the figure so you can determine whether or not your prediction was correct. Your goal is to make as many correct predictions as you can.

On each trial, record on your data sheet the prediction made by the subject immediately after the subject responds. Then show the subject the card representing the "outcome" of that trial. Give the next ready signal after about 3 seconds. Continue at a steady rate until the 100 trials are completed. Be careful to avoid extraneous cues which might affect the subject's prediction. Ask your subject to describe his strategy when his test is completed.

Analysis of data

Divide your data for each subject into four successive blocks of 25 trials (predictions) each. For each block, count the number of predictions of the most frequently reinforced stimulus. (It should be obvious that the number of predictions of the other stimulus will be equal to 25 minus the number of predictions for the most frequently reinforced stimulus, for each block.) Determine the proportion of predictions of the most frequently reinforced stimulus for each block of 25 trials. According to statistical learning theory and the notion of probability matching, this proportion should come closer and closer to the overall probability of its occurrence with each successive block of 25 trials.

Combine your data with those of other members of the class. Determine the mean proportions of predictions of the most frequently reinforced stimulus for each block of 25 trials for the two different reinforcement schedule groups. Plot a graph showing the means of successive blocks for each group. Determine the goodness of fit of the probability matching hypothesis by applying the chi-square test to the predicted and observed mean proportions of responses for the four successive blocks of trials. Apply the test to data for each of the reinforcement schedules separately.

DISCUSSION

1. Do your results indicate probability matching or maximizing of correct predictions? Does the tendency change with each successive block of trials? If so, how?

2. What results would you expect if 1000 trials had been used?

3. What would you expect to find if a 50-50 schedule of reinforcement had been used? Would the results be likely to support probability matching or maximizing of correct predictions?

4. Suppose the subject was informed at the start of the experiment that the sequence of outcomes had been predetermined on a random basis. Would this different procedure lead to different results?

5. Are there clearly different strategies among subjects? If so, are there corresponding differences in performance?

6. What if you had *emphasized* to each subject that "Your goal is to make as many correct predictions as you can."? What if you had repeated this every 25 trials?

REFERENCES

Estes, W. K., & Straughan, J. H. Analysis of verbal conditioning situation in terms of statistical learning theory. *Journal of Experimental Psychology,* 1954, **47**, 225–234.

SELECTED BIBLIOGRAPHY

Bush, R. R., & Mosteller, F. *Stochastic models for learning.* New York: Wiley, 1955.

Estes, W. K. The statistical approach to learning theory. In S. Koch (Ed.), *Psychology: A study of a science,* (Vol. 2). New York: McGraw-Hill, 1959.

Estes, W. K. Probability learning. In A. W. Melton (Ed.), *Categories of human learning.* New York: Academic Press, 1964.

Grant. D. A., Hake, H. W., & Hornseth, J. P. Acquisition and extinction of a verbal conditioned response with differing percentages of reinforcement. *Journal of Experimental Psychology,* 1951, **42,** 1—5.

Humphreys, L. G. Acquisition and extinction of verbal expectations in a situation analogous to conditioning: *Journal of Experimental Psychology,* 1939, **25,** 294—301.

5B
EXPERIMENT
THE GAMBLER'S FALLACY
AS A FUNCTION OF
LENGTH OF EVENT RUNS

Even though the sequence of events in a series may be determined by a randomization procedure, there will be a variety of patterned sub-sequences such as runs of repeated events or alternation of events. The subject may notice these sub-sequences and they may influence his pattern of responding. One pervasive response bias of this sort is the negative recency effect (Jarvik, 1951) which is commonly equated to the phenomenon known as the gambler's fallacy. Suppose you are asked to predict the outcomes of a series of tosses, assuming a fair coin is being used. If a run of consecutive HEADS occurs during the series, you will likely feel more and more certain that TAILS will come up on each successive trials. This subjective bias, that a particular outcome is "overdue," is common even though one knows that the objective probability of each of the two outcomes is 50:50 on a given trial.

Derks (1963) and Goodnow, Rubenstein, and Lubin (1960) have examined the influence of the length of runs on the "gambler's fallacy" in probability learning with 50:50 and other relative proportions of events. They found that with short runs of three or four repeated events, the negative recency effect was strong, but that with long runs of seven or eight or more, there was a shift toward a positive recency effect or a tendency to predict that the run will continue.

Jones and Myers (1966) and Gambino and Myers (1966) have shown that variability of the lengths of runs may be an even more important variable than mean lengths of runs, at least with 50:50 proportions of events. Hence, variability is a factor that must also be considered.

An interesting and relatively simple extension of the binary prediction study would be to examine the influence of mean lengths of runs in a sequence on the negative recency effect. The proportions of predictions of each recurring event outcome can be plotted as a function of consecutive positions in the run sequence. Based on the results of Derks

(1963) and others, the proportion of predictions for recurring events should increase over short run lengths and then begin to decrease for subjects receiving long runs on the average.

REFERENCES

Derks, P. L. Effect of run length on the "gambler's fallacy." *Journal of Experimental Psychology,* 1963, **65**, 213–214.

Gambino, B., & Myers, J. L. Effect of mean and variability of event run length on two-choice learning. *Journal of Experimental Psychology,* 1966, **72**, 904–908.

Goodnow, J. J. Rubenstein, I., & Lubin, A. Response to changing patterns of events. *American Journal of Psychology,* 1960, **73**, 56–67.

Jarvik, M. E. Probability learning and a negative recency effect in the general anticipation of alternative symbols. *Journal of Experimental Psychology,* 1951, **41**, 291–297.

Jones, M. R., & Myers, J. L. A comparison of two methods of event randomization in probability learning. *Journal of Experimental Psychology,* 1966, **72**, 909–911.

DATA SUMMARY ON BINARY PREDICTIONS: PROPORTIONS OF MOST FREQUENTLY REINFORCED RESPONSE

			Schedule A: 80-20		
Trials	1–25	26–50	51–75	76–100	Total
S 1					
2					
3					
4					
5					
Sn					

M

DATA SUMMARY ON BINARY PREDICTIONS: PROPORTIONS OF MOST FREQUENTLY REINFORCED RESPONSE

Schedule B: 60-40

Trials	1–25	26–50	51–75	76–100	Total
S 1					
2					
3					
4					
5					
Sn					
M					

6A
EXPERIMENT
SHORT-TERM MEMORY AS A
FUNCTION OF RETENTION INTERVAL

The classical methods employed in the study of human memory initiated in 1885 by Ebbinghaus deal with relatively long-term memory (LTM). In these studies, the time interval between original learning and the later measure of retention has usually been at least 24 hours. A classic study by Peterson and Peterson (1959) created a great interest in the phenomenon of short-term memory (STM). These investigators demonstrated substantial amounts of forgetting using intervals of 18 seconds or less. In the paradigm they employed, a single trigram (essentially, a three-letter nonsense syllable) was spelled out to the subject. After an interval varying from 3 to 18 seconds, the subject was asked to recall the original trigram. To minimize rehearsal during the retention interval, the subject was required to count backwards by 3's or by 4's from some arbitrarily chosen number given by the experimenter. Peterson and Peterson (1959) found forgetting after even 3 seconds, and the amount of retention loss increased substantially as a direct function of the length of the retention interval.

Are STM and LTM two different phenomena or just the two ends of a continuum? Do the same processes operate in producing forgetting in both situations? To what extent can the memory loss found in the Petersons' paradigm be explained by decay theory versus interference theory? These important theoretical issues were actively pursued following the publication of the Peterson and Peterson (1959) study, as illustrated in Melton's (1963) discussion. This is not the place to present a detailed analysis of these questions, but some mention of the vast theoretical significance placed on STM is necessary to indicate the impact of the Petersons' study. (See also Glanzer & Cunitz, 1966; Keppel & Underwood, 1962; and Postman, 1964).

More recently (e.g., Craik, 1973), criticism has been aimed at the pursuit of this issue that suggests that the distinction between STM and LTM has been taken too literally. Craik argued that instead of regarding STM and LTM as separate entities, it may be more useful to study the levels of processing or the strategies that the subject uses in analyzing the stimuli to be remembered. According to this approach the reason why a given variable such as acoustic similarity of materials affects STM but not LTM, and vice versa for semantic similarity of materials (e.g., Baddeley, 1970), is because the limited time for rehearsal under STM encourages the subject to attend to the sound rather than the meaning of the material. However, these findings should not be used to conclude that two different types of memory store exist. Shulman (1971) and Wickelgren (1973) have pointed out that under the proper conditions subjects will attend to the semantic properties of the material even in STM situations or to acoustic cues even in LTM situations.

The present replication of the Peterson and Peterson study will not shed light on the theoretical issues just described but will provide an opportunity to examine the paradigm that stimulated numerous experiments and models of memory. Their design called for each subject to be tested several times (with different trigrams) after each retention interval. The order in which the different intervals were tested was varied so that there was no systematic pattern. Since each subject was tested at each of the retention intervals, he served, in a sense, as his own control.

METHOD

Subjects

Each experimenter will obtain two subjects. One subject will count backwards by 3's and the other by 4's during the several retention intervals. Determine by some unbiased method which subject will serve under which instruction.

Materials

Forty-eight consonant syllables with an association value of at least 33% are shown in Table 6.1 (from Hilgard, 1951, p. 543). Each syllable is composed of three consonants. The order of the 48 syllables is such that repetition of letters between consecutive trigrams is minimized. In addition to the syllables, Table 6.1 also contains a three-digit number opposite each of the 48 syllables. Half the numbers end with an odd digit and half with an even digit. Counting backwards by 3's is relatively easier for the odd numbers and harder for the even numbers. Conversely, counting backwards by 4's is relatively easier for the even numbers and harder for the odd numbers. Therefore, by having an equal number of odd and even numbers, and by having an equal number of subjects counting backwards by 3's and by 4's, the difficulty of the task interpolated between presentation and recall should be balanced out.

Procedure

After your subject is seated comfortably in a quiet place, read the following instructions:

> I will say three letters, for example, ABC, and then a three-digit number like 309. After I finish giving the number, you are to repeat the *number* immediately and then begin to count backwards by 3's [for one subject, instruct him to count backwards by 3's and for the other subject, by 4's] from that number at a rate of one number per second until I ask you to stop. Stop counting immediately and say the letters that were given at the beginning of the trial. Then there will be a short rest (5 seconds), and a new trial will begin in which I will give you a new set of letters and numbers. Let's try a practice trial. ABC . . . 309. [Stop your subject after 10 seconds.]

Each subject will be tested eight times at each of the six retention intervals, 3, 6, 9, 12, 15, and 18 seconds, a total of 48 trials for each subject. Since a given consonant syllable will be used only once for a given subject, a total of 48 syllables will be required. It should be noted that the 48 syllables in Table 6.1 are divided into eight "blocks" of six syllables each. Within each block of six trials, test your subject once for each length of retention interval. The order of the intervals within each block should be varied from block to block, but the main point is to include each interval only once in each block of six trials. Assign the six blocks in different orders for different subjects.

The experimenter will be left to devise ordering of the intervals within each block and the ordering of the blocks for each of his subjects by suitable randomization procedures. Record the subject's exact responses on test trials in the spaces provided in Table 6.1. Count an omission or "no response" as incorrect.

Analysis of data

Determine the number of correct responses in each retention interval for each subject. Combine these data with those of your classmates and determine the mean number of correct responses for each interval. Prepare a graph depicting the relationship between retention and length of interval.

Compute *t* tests for correlated measures for the mean number of correct responses for each pair of adjacent intervals, i.e., 3 vs. 6, 6 vs. 9, . . . 15 vs. 18. Since five different *t* tests are required, the chances of obtaining a statistically significant difference among the comparisons made are spuriously high. If one computes enough tests, one of them could be significant by chance alone. To keep the overall chance of obtaining a significant difference at an acceptable level (e.g., .05) when multiple comparisons are made, it is possible to use a higher level of significance for each individual test. For example, if .01 is used as the level of significance for each of the five comparisons, the overall probability of obtaining a significant difference by chance alone is close to the commonly accepted level of .05 (.01 x 5). For a more detailed discussion of this problem see Hays (1963, pp. 448–489).

A more detailed analysis of the collated data can be made by performing a block-by-block analysis of the mean number of correct responses for each interval. First, determine separately for the first block of six trials, the mean number of correct responses for all subjects in each interval. Similarly, determine these values for the second and third blocks. Prepare a graph showing retention as a function of interval for each of the three blocks. Analysis of the first three blocks should be sufficient to exhibit evidence of any proactive interference or practice effects, but the student may wish to analyze all eight blocks separately. If learning in the earlier blocks has interfered with learning in the later blocks (proactive interference), the mean number of correct responses should decrease from block to block. If learning in the early blocks has facilitated learning in the later blocks (practice effects), the mean number of correct responses should increase from block to block.

DISCUSSION

1. Does the amount retained vary over the short intervals employed in this experiment? Describe this relationship.

2. Are there any visible differences in the levels or shapes of the retention curves for the first three blocks plotted separately? What explanation can you offer?

3. Do you think the counting numbers backwards task was an effective device to minimize rehearsal during the retention interval? Why or why not? Can you suggest any other means of minimizing rehearsal?

4. Do you think differences in retention would be found between auditory and visual stimulus presentation? Why or why not?

REFERENCES

Baddeley, A. D. Effects of acoustic and semantic similarity on short-term paired-associate learning. *British Journal of Psychology,* 1970, **61,** 335–344.

Craik, F. I. M. A "levels of analysis" view of memory. In P. Pliner, L. Krames & T. Alloway (Eds.) *Communication and affect, language and thought.* New York: Academic Press, 1973.

Glanzer, M., & Cunitz, A. R. Two storage mechanisms in free recall. *Journal of Verbal Learning and Verbal Behavior,* 1966, **5,** 351–360.

Hays, W. L. *Statistics for Psychologists.* New York: Holt, Rinehart, and Winston, 1973.

Hilgard, E. R. Methods and procedures in the study of learning. In S. S. Stevens (Ed.), *Handbook of experimental psychology.* New York: Wiley, 1951.

Keppel, G., & Underwood, B. J. Proactive inhibition in short-term retention of single items. *Journal of Verbal Learning and Verbal Behavior,* 1962, **1,** 153–161.

Melton, A. W. Implications of short-term memory for a general theory of memory. *Journal of Verbal Learning and Verbal Behavior,* 1963, **2,** 1–21.

Peterson, L. R., & Peterson, M. J. Short-term retention of individual verbal items. *Journal of Experimental Psychology,* 1959, **58,** 193–198.

Postman, L. Short-term memory and incidental learning. In A. W. Melton (Ed.), *Categories of human learning.* New York: Academic Press, 1964.

Shulman, H. G. Similarity effects in short-term memory. *Psychological Bulletin,* 1971, **75,** 399–415.

Wickelgren, W. A. The long and the short of memory. *Psychological Bulletin,* 1973, **80,** 425–438.

SELECTED BIBLIOGRAPHY

Keppel, G. Problems of method in the study of the short-term memory. *Psychological Bulletin,* 1965, **63**, 1—13.

TABLE 6.1: STIMULUS SYLLABLES AND NUMBERS

Syllables	Numbers	Retention Interval (Seconds)	S 1	Retention Interval (Seconds)	S 2
1 BFH	415				
2 PGZ	574				
3 RJH	226				
4 QKG	512				
5 CJP	827				
6 BGK	400				
1 SHX	681				
2 DKM	200				
3 TJN	532				
4 CMF	644				
5 GJP	311				
6 FDM	156				
1 HCT	794				
2 JDP	209				
3 ZFT	306				
4 MPB	717				
5 QSG	288				
6 CMZ	619				
1 FNQ	528				
2 SZP	575				
3 DFX	700				
4 NRZ	787				
5 LSH	894				
6 PXT	151				

Syllables	Numbers	Retention Interval (Seconds)	S 1	Retention Interval (Seconds)	S 2
1 GMB	923				
2 TQH	664				
3 JNB	515				
4 HZT	678				
5 QSW	521				
6 ZBK	800				
1 KMX	335				
2 CQK	758				
3 SBF	237				
4 THL	523				
5 XFR	268				
6 BPM	537				
1 KGD	526				
2 RPB	193				
3 MQX	609				
4 ZSN	596				
5 LXH	525				
6 MBS	112				
1 JXC	227				
2 NLR	284				
3 HBK	136				
4 DSZ	415				
5 KPB	171				
6 NCS	395				

6B
EXPERIMENT
SHORT-TERM MEMORY AND THE DIFFICULTY OF THE REHEARSAL PREVENTION TASK

How effective is the rehearsal prevention task in the Peterson and Peterson (1959) type of study? If it is possible for subjects to engage in some rehearsal, then the forgetting of items after a single exposure is not really being measured. If one assumes that the subject's ability to process information is limited, it can be argued that the subject cannot both rehearse the trigram and perform the task of counting backwards at peak levels. To the extent that the subject focuses on one task, his performance on the other task will be less than optimal.

Talland (1967) and Dillon and Reid (1969) compared short-term memory as a function of the type of rehearsal prevention task. They found that the more demanding the type of rehearsal prevention task, the poorer the short-term memory. The results of these investigators are consistent with the view that when confronted with two tasks, better performance on one may lead to poorer performance on the other (Crowder, 1967; Johnston, Greenberg, Fisher, & Martin, 1970).

As a possible extension to Experiment 6A, a comparison could be made of two different types of rehearsal prevention activity to see if there is an inverse relationship between short-term memory and the difficulty of the rehearsal prevention task.

It would not be necessary to employ all of the original time intervals. One group of subjects could be given an easy task, such as classification of numbers as odd or even, while the other group might be required to count backwards by 3's. A comparison could be made of the mean number of correctly recalled trigrams for the two different groups at each retention interval used.

REFERENCES

Crowder, R. G. Short-term memory for words with a perceptual-motor interpolated activity. *Journal of Verbal Learning and Verbal Behavior,* 1967, **6**, 753–761.

Dillon, R. F., & Reid, L. S. Short-term memory as a function of information processing during the retention interval. *Journal of Experimental Psychology,* 1969, **81**, 261–269.

Johnston, W. A., Greenberg, S. N., Fisher, R. P., & Martin, D. W. Divided attention: A vehicle of monitoring memory processes. *Journal of Experimental Psychology,* 1970, **83**, 164–171.

Peterson, L. R., & Peterson, M. J. Short-term retention of individual verbal items. *Journal of Experimental Psychology,* 1959, **58**, 193–198

Talland, G. A. Short-term memory with interpolated activity. *Journal of Verbal Learning and Verbal Behavior,* 1967, **6**, 144–150.

DATA SUMMARY ON SHORT-TERM MEMORY: NUMBER OF CORRECT RESPONSES RETENTION INTERVAL (SECONDS)

	3	6	9	12	15	18
S 1						
2						
3						
4						
5						
Sn						
M						
SD						

7A
EXPERIMENT
VERBAL CONDITIONING AND AWARENESS AS A FUNCTION OF INSTRUCTIONAL SET

In any interpersonal situation many subtle forms of verbal reinforcement may occur without any given person being aware of the process. That is, by some form of verbal approval, e.g., "good," "mm-hmm," "yes," etc., it is conceivable that some aspect of the verbal behavior of a person is reinforced by the experimenter) some form of verbal reinforcement was Kanfer (1968) provided an analysis of the development of research on this topic and its significance.

One of the first pieces of experimental support for the existence of the phenomenon of verbal conditioning was found by Greenspoon (1955) who differentially reinforced singular and plural words. Subjects were instructed to say words as they came to mind. While they were responding, the experimenter murmured "mm-hmm" after all plural words for one group and after all singular words for a different group. A third group which did not receive this form of verbal reinforcement served as the control group. Greenspoon found evidence of verbal conditioning in the group reinforced for plural words but not in the group reinforced for singular words. Greenspoon's control group (no reinforcement) showed that singular words are emitted much more frequently than plural words. Hence, one explanation of the failure to influence the number of singular words by verbal reinforcement is simply that there is little room for an increase in this already strong tendency.

A more structured task was used by Taffel (1955). He presented verbs in the simple past tense typed one to a card in conjunction with the six personal pronouns. The task required subjects to compose sentences using each verb in conjunction with any one of the six pronouns. As in the Greenspoon study, the subjects were not told the true reason for the study but were told that the experimenter was actually interested in some other purpose, e.g., to see how people make sentences. After a certain class of sentences (those starting with the arbitrarily chosen pronoun to be reinforced by the experimenter), some form of verbal reinforcement was

given. Evidence of verbal conditioning was shown when the proportion of sentences starting with the reinforced pronoun increased during the experiment while the proportion of those starting with nonreinforced pronouns did not.

Numerous experiments on verbal conditioning have been conducted employing different tasks, types of reinforcers, types of reinforced responses, etc. (For excellent reviews, see Krasner, 1958, 1967.) While some of these studies found evidence of verbal conditioning, others did not. Some studies (De Nike, 1964; Levin, 1961; Spielberger, 1962; Spielberger & Levin, 1962) suggest that one important consideration is the *level of awareness* of the subject. It has often been assumed that demonstrations of verbal conditioning illustrate the occurrence of learning without awareness. However, increasing evidence (Dulany, 1962; Farber, 1963; Spielberger, 1965) suggests that subjects who exhibit verbal conditioning are usually "aware" of the contingencies between verbal response and reinforcement, and that those who are "unaware" usually fail to condition. "Awareness" in this situation is defined as the subject's ability to state the response-reinforcement contingency when questioned during a post-experimental interview.

An interesting experiment (Spielberger & Levin, 1962) examined the effect of varying instructional sets on verbal conditioning in the Taffel task. These experimenters told one group that they were interested in how people make up sentences, and a second group that some sentences are better than others, that is, that there was some preferred type of sentence which they should be composing. A greater percentage of the subjects in the latter group showed awareness of the response-reinforcement contingency during the postexperimental interview. In addition, a higher level of conditioning was obtained with the instructed group.

This experiment utilizes a similar modification of the Taffel technique to examine the relationship between verbal conditioning and level of awareness and the effects of instructions on both.

METHOD

Subjects

Each experimenter will obtain three subjects preferably *not* from among his friends and acquaintances. Assign one subject to each of the three conditions, Informed, Uninformed, and Control, by some unbiased procedure. Try to restrict subjects to a narrow range of age (to be determined more explicitly in class).

Materials

One hundred 3 x 5 cards or slips of paper will be needed to present the verbs. On a separate card typed in a center row, there should appear the six personal pronouns: I, YOU, WE, SHE, HE, THEY. A different verb of the simple past tense should be typed in the center of each of the 100 cards. The 100 verbs to be used are arbitrary but are commonly used verbs in the language. (See Table 7.1 for list of verbs.)

Procedure

Testing sessions should be conducted in a room free from distraction. Insofar as the experimenter is attempting to influence the behavior of the subject by subtle means, it is extremely important that the experimenter be very careful in following instructions explicitly, and in avoiding any side remarks, comments, and socializing during the conditioning session. After seating the subject, explain briefly that the instructions will be read and that the subject should pay close attention. Allow him to ask questions of clarification or repetition but say nothing regarding the nature or purpose of the experiment. Tell the subject he can ask any other questions after the experiment.

The instructions for the *Uninformed* and *Control* groups are as follows:

> The purpose of this experiment is to study how people make up sentences. I will show you a number of slips of paper each of which contains a single verb in the simple past tense typed in the center. You are to make up any sentence which you can think of, using the verb on each slip starting with *any one* of the pronouns on *this card* [present card to the subject containing six personal pronouns and leave it in front of him during the entire experiment]. It doesn't matter whether your sentence is long or short, true or false, simple or complicated, but it is important that you answer with the first sentence which enters your mind. At first you may find this difficult but as we continue it will become easier so don't feel discouraged. Remember, make up the first sentence you can think of, starting with one of the pronouns on the card before you and including the verb typed on each slip presented to you.

For the *Informed* group, use the following instructions:

> The purpose of this experiment is to study how people make up sentences. I will show you a number of slips of paper each of which

contains a single verb in the simple past tense typed in the center. You are to make up a sentence using the verb on each slip starting with *any one* of the pronouns on this card [present card to the subject containing six personal pronouns and leave it in front of him during the entire experiment]. The type of sentence you construct is important; some sentences are better than others. Try to discover which sentences are better. Remember, make up the *best* sentence which comes to mind, starting with one of the pronouns on the card before you and including the verb typed on each slip presented to you.

Shuffle the deck of verbs for each subject to provide a different order of verb presentation for each one. Each slip should be placed in front of your subject, one at a time, keeping the rest of the deck out of view. When your subject has responded, record the pronoun used on the data sheet. It is not necessary to record the entire sentence. However, be sure that the data sheet is kept out of the subject's view so that he will not become suspicious owing to the recording of only the pronoun.

Verbal conditioning groups

In this experiment the pronoun "They" will be reinforced. One could choose any other pronoun desired. Different pronouns have different base rates of usage. The pronoun "They" has a relatively low base rate which provides the opportunity to increase usage with conditioning. The verbal expression to be used will be a murmur of "mm-hmm" in a neutral tone on reinforced trials. Other expressions such as "good" could be substituted.

During all 100 trials, record the pronoun used and give the verbal reinforcer at the end of each sentence in which your subject used the pronoun "They." Be careful that you do not reinforce inappropriate sentences. Then present the next slip to your subject and proceed in the same fashion.

Control group

During all 100 trials or verbs, do not give reinforcement after any sentence. Merely record the pronoun used. Then present the next slip to your subject.

Interview

A series of open-ended questions will be asked of all subjects after the 100 trials have been completed. They will be general at first and become increasingly specific in an attempt to assess the degree of the subject's awareness of what was going on in the experiment. However, they should not suggest to the subject that anything other than the stated purpose of the experiment was involved. For example, the first question should be "What do you think was the purpose of the experiment?" and *not* "Did you know that I said something after each sentence you made starting with 'They'?" Below are some interview questions:

1. What do you think was the purpose of the experiment?
2. Did you notice anything unusual during the experiment?
3. Did you notice anything I said during the experiment? [If the answer is yes, ask the following] : What exactly? When did you first notice it? [If the subject answers "no" to 2 and 3, classify the subject as Unaware and terminate your interview.]
4. Actually I said "mm-hmm" from time to time. Why do you think I made those comments during the experiment? Do you think they were a part of the experiment? In what way? [If answers to above questions suggest that the subject knows the contingency between reinforcement and response, classify the subject as Aware. If, on the other hand, answers to these questions suggest that the subject noticed your comments but did not perceive the correlation between responses and verbal reinforcement, classify the subject as Unaware and terminate your interview.]
5. What did you do during the experiment as a result of noticing the comments I made?

These interviews are usually conducted and/or rated by independent raters. Since no provision has been made here for this, the experimenter must be careful to avoid letting his knowledge of the condition under which the subject served influence his judgment concerning the subject's awareness.

After the interview is concluded, explain the purpose of the experiment to each subject.

Analysis of data

Determine for each subject the number of sentences beginning with the reinforced pronoun (They) for each block of 20 successive trials. Combine your results with those of your classmates for each experimental condition.

In arranging your data for the Informed and Uninformed conditions, group separately the results for subjects classified as "Aware" and "Unaware" on the basis of the interview.

Present graphically the mean number of sentences starting with "They" for each of the following groups: Control, Informed-Aware, Informed-Unaware, Uninformed-Aware, and Uninformed-Unaware.

Arbitrarily choose one of the five nonreinforced pronouns for the same analysis. Determine how frequently this pronoun occurred for each block of 20 trials for each of the five groups above and present these results graphically. Compare trends for this pronoun and for "They."

Compare the results for "They" in the Control condition with those of all subjects in the Informed condition. Make the same comparison between the Control and Uninformed conditions. Now compare the combined results of all Aware subjects with those of the combined results of all Unaware subjects. Similarly, compare results of the Control condition separately with those of the Aware and Unaware subjects.

Perform *t* tests for independent observations on differences in mean total sentences starting with "They" for Control versus Informed, Control versus Uninformed, Informed versus Uninformed. Similarly test the differences between Control versus Aware, Control versus Unaware, and Aware versus Unaware. Compare the percentages of subjects in each of the Informed and Uninformed conditions who are judged Aware versus Unaware. (See Experiment 6A, *Analysis of data*, for discussion of significance levels to be used.)

DISCUSSION

1. Do the results support the existence of learning without awareness?

2. If the evidence shows that Aware subjects condition better than Unaware subjects, does this mean that learning is caused by awareness or that awareness is caused by learing? How does one decide between these two alternatives?

3. Is it more useful to dichotomize awareness versus unawareness or to consider awareness-unawareness as a continuum with varying levels of gradations?

4. Comparisons based on all 100 trials may yield different results from those based on some smaller portions of the trials, for example, the last block of 20 trials. Why? Test any differences between conditions over a limited number of trials if it appears that different conclusions might arise than from those based on all 100 trials.

5. In reference to interview question 5, were there differences in what subjects reported having done as a result of noticing the experimenter's comments? If so, how could your results have been influenced?

6. Do you think the postexperimental interview is an adequate procedure for assessing awareness?

REFERENCES

De Nike, L. D. The temporal relationship between awareness and performance in verbal conditioning. *Journal of Experimental Psychology,* 1964, **68,** 521–529.

Dulany, D. E., Jr. The place of hypotheses and intentions: An analysis of verbal control in verbal conditioning. In C. W. Eriksen (Ed.), *Behavior and awareness—a symposium of research and interpretation.* Durham, N. C.: Duke University Press, 1962, pp. 102–129.

Farber, I. E. The things people say to themselves. *American Psychologist,* 1963, **18,** 185–197.

Greenspoon, J. The reinforcing effect of two spoken sounds on the frequency of two responses. *American Journal of Psychology,* 1955, **68,** 409–416.

Kanfer, F. H. Verbal conditioning: A review of its status. In T. R. Dixon & D. L. Horton (Eds.), *Verbal behavior and general behavior theory.* Englewood Cliffs, N. J.: Prentice-Hall, 1968.

Krasner, L. Studies of the conditioning of verbal behavior. *Psychological Bulletin,* 1958, **55,** 148–170.

Krasner, L. Verbal operant conditioning and awareness. In K. Salzinger & S. Salzinger (Eds.), *Research in verbal behavior and some neurophysiological implications.* New York: Academic Press, 1967.

Levin, S. M. The effects of awareness on verbal conditioning. *Journal of Experimental Psychology,* 1961, **61,** 67–75.

Spielberger, C. D. The role of awareness in verbal conditioning. In C. W. Eriksen (Ed.), *Behavior and awareness—A symposium of research and interpretation.* Durham, N. C.; Duke University Press, 1962.

Spielberger, C. D. Theoretical and epistemological issues in verbal conditioning. In S. Rosenberg (Ed.), *Directions in psycholinguistics.* New York: Macmillan, 1965.

Spielberger, C. D., & Levin, S. M. What is learned in verbal conditioning? *Journal of Verbal Learning & Verbal Behavior,* 1962, **1**, 125–132.

Taffel, C. Anxiety and the conditioning of verbal behavior. *Journal of Abnormal and Social Psychology,* 1955, **51**, 496–501.

7B
EXPERIMENT
EVALUATION APPREHENSION
AND VERBAL CONDITIONING

The verbal conditioning paradigm is an ambiguous task from the point of view of the subject. The manner in which he performs may be affected by his hypotheses about the purpose of the task and his views as to what type of performance might be considered as appropriate. Orne (1962) referred to the subject's perceptions as the demand characteristics of the situation. He suggested that most subjects are prone to be highly cooperative, especially if they are volunteers. Orne suggested that subjects will try to please the experimenter by performing in a manner that they think will verify the experimenter's hypotheses. These attitudes should facilitate verbal conditioning in subjects.

Rosenberg (1969) emphasized the fact that most subjects are apprehensive when placed in an evaluation situation, such as a psychological experiment, because they would not like to be judged unfavorably. According to Sigall, Aronson, and Van Hoose (1970), if the situation is such that the subject must choose between "looking good" and "looking bad" just to satisfy the experimenter's expectancies, he will act to enhance his own appearance. Lichenstein and Craine (1967) have also shown how the importance of verbal reinforcers to a subject can vary and modify the amount of verbal conditioning.

Page (1971) examined the influence of evaluation apprehension on verbal conditioning. In his study, he gave a pretest that allegedly measured conformity. Assuming that subjects would be sensitized to the issue of conformity and that they would wish to avoid being judged as conformist, Page hypothesized that they would try to avoid verbal reinforcement on the conditioning task. Compared to a control group that did not receive the fake pretest of conformity, there was less verbal conditioning, thus confirming Page's hypothesis. These results are more consistent with the position of Sigall, Aronson, and Van Hoose (1970) than with that of Orne (1962).

An extension of the verbal conditioning experiment might be based on the Page study which manipulated evaluation apprehension.

REFERENCES

Lichenstein, E., & Craine, W. H. The importance of subjective evaluation of reinforcement in verbal conditioning. *Journal of Experimental Research in Personality,* 1967, **3**, 214–220.

Orne, M. T. On the social psychology of the psychological experiment: With particular reference to demand characteristics and their implications. *American Psychologist,* 1962, **17**, 776–783.

Page, M. M. Effects of evaluation apprehension on cooperation in verbal conditioning. *Journal of Experimental Research in Personality,* 1971, **5**, 85–91.

Rosenberg, M. J. The conditions and consequences of evaluation apprehension. In R. Rosenthal, & R. L. Rosnow (Eds.) *Artifact in behavioral research.* New York: Academic Press, 1969.

Sigall, H., Aronson, E., & Van Hoose, T. The cooperative subject: Myth or reality. *Journal of Experimental and Social Psychology,* 1970, **6**, 1–10.

TABLE 7.1:   ONE HUNDRED SIMPLE PAST TENSE VERBS

acted	drank	liked	scraped
aimed	dreamed	listened	scratched
arrived	drew	lived	screamed
ate	dropped	looked	shook
baked	drove	lost	shouted
believed	dug	loved	slept
bent	enjoyed	missed	smiled
blew	fastened	moved	sneezed
bought	fell	painted	sold
broiled	fixed	planned	started
broke	flew	played	steered
brought	fought	pointed	stopped
built	found	prayed	studied
burned	frowned	pulled	talked
came	gave	punished	tied
caught	grew	pushed	tipped
climbed	grieved	put	took
colored	guided	ran	turned
cooked	hated	read	twisted
coughed	hiked	rewarded	walked
counted	jumped	rolled	watched
crawled	kicked	said	went
cried	knew	sang	won
cut	laughed	saved	wrote
died	lifted	saw	yawned

DATA SUMMARY ON VERBAL CONDITIONING: NUMBER OF CORRECT RESPONSES (PER BLOCK OF 20 TRIALS)

	I	II	III	IV	V	Σ			I	II	III	IV	V	Σ			I	II	III	IV	V	Σ
_S_ 1								_S_ 1								_S_ 1						
2								2								2						
3								3								3						
4								4								4						
5								5								5						
_Sn_																						

Column group headers:
- Uninformed Group / Unaware _S_s
- Informed Group / Unaware _S_s
- Control Group

M　　　　　　　　　　　M　　　　　　　　　　　M

SD　　　　　　　　　　SD　　　　　　　　　　SD

DATA SUMMARY ON VERBAL CONDITIONING: NUMBER OF CORRECT RESPONSES (PER BLOCK OF 20 TRIALS)

		Uninformed Group Aware Ss						Informed Group Aware Ss					
	I	II	III	IV	V	Σ		I	II	III	IV	V	Σ
S 1							S 1						
2							2						
3							3						
4							4						
5							5						
Sn							Sn						
M							M						
SD							SD						

8A
EXPERIMENT
SERIAL POSITION CURVE IN FREE RECALL VERSUS SERIAL RECALL

When a serial list of verbal materials is read once to a subject and the task required is the *free recall* of the words in any order, it has been found (Deese & Kaufman, 1957) that the most frequently recalled words are those at the end of the list followed by those at the beginning and finally those in the middle. This is in contrast to the serial position curve typically found under *serial anticipation learning*, where the subject must anticipate in serial order (e.g., Ward, 1937). In this situation the items which are at the beginning of the list are most frequently recalled, followed by those at the end, with those in the middle being poorest. Thus, depending on whether *anticipation learning* or *free recall* is required, different serial position curves are obtained.

One might ask what the form of the serial position curve would be on a serial recall task in which the subject is asked to *recall* rather than *anticipate* in serial order a list which had been presented once to him? Would it be more like the *serial anticipation learning* or the *free recall* curve? According to Jahnke (1963) when *serial recall* is required, the serial position curve is more similar to the one for *serial anticipation learning*.

The goal of this study is to compare recall of serial lists of verbal materials as a function of (a) *free recall* and (b) *serial recall*. Thus it compares the type of recall required in the Deese and Kaufman (1957) study with that studied by Jahnke (1963).

METHOD

Subjects

Each experimenter should obtain four subjects, two for each of the two conditions. Devise some unbiased system for assigning subjects to the two conditions.

Materials

Fifteen words from the Thorndike-Lorge Word Count (1944), which occur between 900 and 1100 times per 4½ million words in the written English language will be used. Words of about equal length were selected, and no two words start with the same letter: HAT, YEAR, FOOD, JOB, ARM, WAR, DAY, BIRD, KNEE, USE, MAN, TIME, ROSE, PASS, NOTE.

Procedure

After seating the subject in a place free from distraction, you should read the appropriate set of instructions:

Free recall condition. This is a simple memory test. I am going to read you a list of 15 words at a rate of about one word per second. Please listen closely since I cannot repeat any word. After you have heard the list I will give you a slip of lined paper on which I want you to write as many of the words as you can recall *in any order*. Start at the top line and do not skip any lines.

Serial recall condition. This is a simple memory test. I am going to read you a list of 15 words at a rate of about one word per second. Please listen closely since I cannot repeat any word. After you have heard the list I will give you a slip of lined paper on which I want you to write as many of the words as you can recall in *exactly the same order* in which they were read to you.

After giving the appropriate instructions, read the list to the subject. Use a different serial order of presentation of the list for each subject. Keep a record of the presentation orders for use in scoring subjects' responses. Then give the subject a slip of paper with 15 unnumbered blank lines drawn horizontally across the page. Allow the subject 60 seconds for recall.

Analysis of data

Determine the number of correct responses for each subject. For the free recall condition, simply determine the number correctly recalled. For the serial recall condition, scoring is somewhat more complicated. A stringent criterion for serial recall is to count as correct only those words recalled which were written in exactly the same ordinal position as they were read. However, it is possible that a subject may recall a number of words in correct order relative to each other but may place them incorrectly as far as the exact ordinal position in which they were read. For example, suppose a subject recalls the 5th, 6th, 7th, and 8th items in order but writes them on the 1st, 2nd, 3rd, and 4th lines on the data sheet. Are these responses correct or incorrect? They are incorrect by a stringent criterion, but by a more lenient criterion they could be counted as correct. Score your serial recall data by *both criteria*. In using the stringent criterion, count a word correct only if it is recalled in the exact ordinal position in which it was read; in using the lenient criterion, score a word correct if it is recalled immediately after a word which it actually followed during the list presentation. For example, if a subject gives the 4th, 12th, 13th, and 6th items as his first four words on serial recall, score the 13th word as correct since it is given in recall after the word it actually had followed originally, i.e., the 12th word.

Amount of recall

Determine the mean number of correctly recalled words for the combined class data for each of the two conditions. Compare the recall for the serial and the free recall conditions. Compute a *t* test between the mean number of correct responses for the serial and free recall conditions.

Serial position curves

From the combined class data, determine the percentage of subjects getting an item correct at each serial position for each of the two conditions. Plot a serial position curve for each type of recall.

Temporal order of recall

For the free recall condition, determine the order in which free recall occurred as a function of serial presentation order for the combined class data. Determine the magnitude of the relationship between the order of recall of each item and the frequency with which it was recalled by computing a rank order correlation between the mean temporal order of recall and the proportion of subjects who recalled each item in the list.

DISCUSSION

1. How does the type of recall task affect the number of items recalled?

2. Compare visually the serial position curves obtained as a function of the type of task.

3. For the free recall condition, is the order of recall related to the number of items recalled? Compare serial position of presentation and temporal order of recall.

4.   Do you think the serial position curves would be different if nonsense syllables had been used instead of words?

REFERENCES

Deese, J., & Kaufman, R. A. Serial effects in recall of unorganized and sequentially organized verbal material *Journal of Experimental Psychology,* 1957, **54,** 180–187.

Jahnke, J. C. Serial position effects in immediate free recall. *Journal of Verbal Learning and Verbal Behavior,* 1963, **2,** 284–287.

Thorndike, E. L., & Lorge, I. *The teacher's word book of 30,000 words.* New York: Teachers College, Columbia University, 1944.

Ward, L. B. Reminiscence and rote learning. *Psychological Monographs,* 1937, **49,** No. 220.

SELECTED BIBLIOGRAPHY

Deese, J. Frequency of usage and number of words in free recall: The role of association. *Psychological Reports,* 1960, **7,** 337–344.

Jahnke, J. C. Supplementary report: Primacy and recency effects in serial-position curves of immediate recall. *Journal of Experimental Psychology,* 1965, **70,** 130–132.

Murdock, B. B., Jr. The immediate retention of unrelated words. *Journal of Experimental Psychology,* 1960, **64,** 222–234.

Waugh, N. C. Free versus serial recall. *Journal of Experimental Psychology* 1961, **62,** 496–502.

8B
EXPERIMENT
SHORT-TERM STORAGE AND
LONG-TERM STORAGE

Theoretical interest in the processes underlying the shape of the serial position curve obtained with free recall has led to the examination of the influence of several variables on the curve (Glanzer & Cunitz, 1966; Glanzer & Schwartz, 1971; Murdock, 1962; Postman & Phillips, 1965; and Waugh & Norman, 1965). In essence, it has been suggested that the serial position curve in free recall is the composite of two components, short-term and long-term storage, which are affected by different variables. The recency effect, or better recall of items at the end of the list, is attributed primarily to short-term store, whereas the recall of earlier items in the list are presumed to reflect primarily long-term store.

Accordingly, it has been proposed that certain variables such as presentation rate and length of list will influence the beginning of the curve, which reflects primarily long-term store. However, they should not affect the end of the curve, which represents primarily short-term store. The reverse is hypothesized for variables such as delay between input and recall that should affect the long-term store (beginning of curve). Glanzer and Cunitz (1966) tested these predictions successfully.

It might be added that there is some disagreement (Gruneberg, 1970, 1972) concerning the conclusiveness of findings, such as those of Glanzer and Cunitz (1966), who interpret them as proof of the existence of two separate memory mechanisms. According to Gruneberg, the observed impairment of recall of items at the end of the list when a delay is imposed might merely reflect the fact that rehearsal of these items is prevented rather than constituting evidence that short- and long-term memory involve different mechaniisms. As an extension to Experiment 8A, it might be instructive to compare free recall curves immediately after input and after several delay lengths. According to Glanzer and Cunitz (1966), recency effects or recall of items at the end of the list should be stronger with immediate recall but there should be no differences in recall of items at the start of the list as a function of the delay interval.

REFERENCES

Glanzer, M., & Cunitz, A. R. Two storage mechanisms in free recall. *Journal of Verbal Learning and Verbal Behavior,* 1966, **5,** 351–360.

Glanzer, M., & Schwartz, A. Mnemonic structure in free recall; differential effects on STS and LTS. *Journal of Verbal Learning and Verbal Behavior,* 1971, **10,** 194–198.

Gruneberg, M. M. A dichotomous theory of memory—unproved and unprovable. *Acta Psychologica,* 1970, **34,** 489–496.

Gruneburg, M. M. The serial position curve and the distinction between short- and long-term memory. *Acta Psychologica,* 1972, **36,** 221–225.

Murdock, B. B., Jr. The serial position effect of free recall. *Journal of Experimental Psychology,* 1962, **64,** 482–488.

Postman, L., & Phillips, L. W. Short-term temporal changes in free recall. *Quarterly Journal of Experimental Psychology,* 1965, **17,** 132–138.

Waugh, N. C., & Norman, D. A. Primary memory. *Psychological Review,* 1965, **72,** 89–104.

DATA SUMMARY ON FREE AND SERIAL RECALL: NUMBER OF CORRECT RECALLS

	Free Recall		Serial Recall	
	Lenient Criterion	Stringent Criterion	Lenient Criterion	Stringent Criterion
S 1				
2				
3				
4				
5				
S_n				

M

SD

9A
EXPERIMENT
ROLE OF STORAGE AND
RETRIEVAL CUES ON MEMORY

What happens to material that we cannot remember? Is it truly forgotten and gone forever, or is it only momentarily lost? By using retrieval cues, Tulving and Pearlstone (1967) have shown that material that was assumed forgotten or not available could, in fact, be recalled or made accessible. Similarly, many persons experience difficulty in remembering at times, only to find later that under other conditions the same material is easily recalled. Apparently some external cues act to jog or trigger our memories, so to speak.

In order to have more control over the operation of these cues, Tulving and Osler (1968) presented a list of 24 unrelated words to subjects to memorize. The total design employed 19 conditions, but for our purposes we will need to examine only four of them. Half the subjects received a verbal cue along with each word while the other half did not. The cues were low associates of the words in the list but were assumed to serve as possible aids to memory. At recall, each group was divided so that half of the subjects received the cues as possible aids and half did not.

The four conditions can be summarized as follows: (a) cues at both input and output (CC), (b) cues at input but not at output (CNC), (c) no cues at input but cues at output (NCC), and (d) no cues at either input or output (NCNC). Tulving and Osler (1968) predicted and found that Group CC recalled more words than Group NCNC. Less clear expectancies existed concerning the other two conditions. They were included to determine whether cues given only at input or only at output would result in better performance than that in the NCNC condition. Results showed that recall under these intermediate conditions was no better, and in fact, slightly poorer than that obtained in the NCNC condition. The indication was that cues are not beneficial for recall unless they appear both at input and output.

The present study is based on the portion of the Tulving and Osler (1968) study described above, and examines the effects of cues on recall.

METHOD

Subjects

Each experimenter will obtain four subjects, one for each condition. Devise some unbiased method of assigning subjects to the four conditions and the order of testing.

Materials

Table 9.1 contains a list of 24 words from the Kent-Rosanoff (1910) word association list and one low frequency (between 1% and 7%) associate for each word. Copy each of the 24 words on a separate card with the corresponding low frequency associate on the back side.

Procedure

The words to be recalled will be presented visually to the subjects at a 4-second rate of presentation. For the cued input conditions (CC, CNC), the experimenter will also pronounce the corresponding low frequency associate that is assumed to serve as the retrieval cue at recall.

Read the following instructions to all your subjects before presenting the words:

TABLE 9.1: STIMULUS WORDS AND LOW ASSOCIATE RETRIEVAL CUES

TABLE	(desk)	DREAM	(nightmare)
DARK	(room)	LIGHT	(bright)
BLACK	(cat)	SWIFT	(river)
SLOW	(stop)	LONG	(narrow)
GIRL	(friend)	BITTER	(taste)
HIGH	(mountain)	SQUARE	(block)
HARD	(easy)	BED	(sheet)
EAGLE	(scout)	HEAVY	(hold)
HOUSE	(garage)	SCISSORS	(paper)
ROUGH	(road)	SALT	(water)
ANGER	(hate)	KING	(crown)
SOUR	(lemon)	TOBACCO	(pipe)

Note: Stimulus words shown in upper case, cues in lower case.

This is a study of factors affecting memory. I will show you a series of 24 unrelated words which I want you to read silently and try and remember because I will ask you to recall them afterwards. I will show you each word on a separate card for about 4 seconds each.

For the subjects in the cued input (CC and CNC) conditions, read the following additional instructions:

> As an aid to your memory, I will say a word aloud as I show each of the 24 words to be recalled. Use these spoken words as hints if you can, but you will not have to recall them later.

Provide answer sheets with 24 blank spaces for all subjects. For the cued output conditions (CC, NCC) the answer sheets will include the 24 low frequency associates in a single column in an order that is different from the one used during input. Allow 5 minutes for written recall for all conditions.

Take a 30-second break after the last word is presented before testing for recall. Then provide the subject with the appropriate answer sheet and read the appropriate instructions for recall:

For the noncued output conditions (CNCN, NCNC):

> You may have 5 minutes to recall as many of the words which I showed you on the cards as you can. You may write them down in any order.

For the cued output conditions (CC, NCC):

> Here is a list of 24 words that might be helpful hints to aid your recall of the words that I showed you on the cards. You may have 5 minutes to recall as many of the words on the cards as you can. You may write them down in any order.

At the end of the 5 minute recall period, take the answer sheet, interrogate your subject concerning any strategies that may have been used, whether the intended cues were helpful, and answer any questions that your subject may have about the experiment.

Analysis of data

Determine the number of correctly recalled words for each of the four conditions. Compute a 2 x 2 (input cues by output cues) analysis of variance for independent measures on these data. If any of the F values are significant, perform the appropriate pairwise comparisons between means using t tests for independent measures. Also record the number of incorrectly recalled words (not including omissions) in each condition.

DISCUSSION

1. What conclusions can you draw about the usefulness of the cues given during input? During output?

2. Were cues useful if provided only at input but not at output? How might they have been a source of interference? Were any cue words incorrectly recalled in the CNC condition?

3. Were cues helpful if introduced only at output, that is, the NCC condition?

4. What strategies did any of your subjects report using? What did they report about the use of cues?

REFERENCES

Kent, G. H., & Rosanoff, A. J. A study of association in insanity. *American Journal of Insanity,* 1910, **67**, 37–96, 317– 390.

Tulving, E., & Osler, S. Effectiveness of retrieval cues in memory for words. *Journal of Experimental Psychology,* 1968, **77**, 593–601.

Tulving, E., & Pearlstone, Z. Availability versus accessibility of information in memory of words. *Journal of Verbal Learning and Verbal Behavior,* 1966, **5**, 381–391.

SELECTED BIBLIOGRAPHY

Earhard, M. Storage and retrieval of words encoded in memory. *Journal of Experimental Psychology,* 1969, **80**, 412–418.

Funkhouser, G. R. Effects of differential encoding on recall. *Journal of Verbal Learning and Verbal Behavior,* 1968, **7**, 1016–1023.

Light, L. L. Homonyms and synonyms as retrieval cues. *Journal of Experimental Psychology,* 1972, **96**, 255–262.

Thomson, D. M., & Tulving, E. Associative encoding and retrieval: Weak and strong cues. *Journal of Experimental Psychology,* 1970, **86**, 255–262.

9B
EXPERIMENT
RETRIEVAL FROM MEMORY AS A FUNCTION OF WEAK VS. STRONG ASSOCIATION CUES

One might conclude from the Tulving and Osler (1968) study that retrieval cues must be paired with the words to be recalled during input if they are to be effective during output. This view is termed the encoding specificity hypothesis by Thomson and Tulving (1970) and Tulving and Thomson (1973), and it can be contrasted with a view that they refer to as the associative continuity hypothesis. Under the latter notion, any cue that has strong preexperimental association with a word to be recalled should be successful as a retrieval cue even if it had not been presented during the input stage of the experiment. Thus, TABLE should elicit CHAIR on the basis of its being a strong preexperimental associate and it need not have been actually paired with CHAIR during the experiment. The work of Bahrick (1969, 1970) and Fox, Blick, and Bilodeau (1964) have demonstrated support for this view.

On the other hand, one test by Thomson and Tulving (1970) favored their prediction, namely that a cue must be specifically paired and encoded with a word if that cue is to be effective in aiding retrieval during output. In part of their study, they first gave subjects lists of words to be recalled and along with each word, a weak associate was presented to serve as an encoding cue. Then, some subjects received those same weak associates as retrieval cues at recall, while others received stronger associates that had not previously appeared in the experiment as their retrieval cues. Better recall occurred with the original weak retrieval cues than with the strong retrieval cues when the weak cues had been provided for encoding, suggesting that the original encoding offset the strong preexperimental associations as retrieval cues. However, when the stronger cues were provided for the first time at retrieval, still better recall was obtained. In other conditions in which weak cues were provided only at input or only at output, performance was poorer than when no cues were provided at either time, suggesting that weak cues must be available at both input and output to be effective retrieval aids.

An extension of the study of cueing on recall could incorporate one or more portions of the Thomson and Tulving (1970) study by comparing recall as a function of the associative strength of retrieval cues.

REFERENCES

Bahrick, H. P. Measurement of memory by prompted recall. *Journal of Experimental Psychology,* 1969, **79,** 213–219.

Bahrick, H. P. Two-phase model for prompted recall. *Psychological Review,* 1970, **77,** 215–222.

Fox, P. W., Blick, K. A., & Bilodeau, E. A. Stimulation and prediction of verbal recall and misrecall. *Journal of Experimental Psychology,* 1964, **68,** 321–322.

Thomson, D. M., & Tulving, E. Associative encoding and retrieval: Weak and strong cues. *Journal of Experimental Psychology,* 1970, **86,** 255–262.

Tulving, E., & Osler, S. Effectiveness of retrieval cues in memory for words. *Journal of Experimental Psychology,* 1968, **77,** 593–601.

Tulving, E., & Thomson, D. M. Encoding specificity and retrieval processes in episodic memory. *Psychological Reports,* 1973, **80,** 352–373.

DATA SUMMARY ON CUEING AND RECALL: NUMBER OF WORDS RECALLED

Condition

	CC		CNC		NCC		NCNC	
	Correct	Errors	Correct	Errors	Correct	Errors	Correct	Errors
S 1								
2								
3								
4								
5								
S_n								

M
SD

10 A
EXPERIMENT
THE EFFECTS OF
CODING ON MEMORY

When a person is required to memorize material, it is not uncommon for him to devise and employ so-called mnemonic devices to aid in the storage and recall of the material. In experiments on memory, for example, how does the subject memorize a nonsense syllable? At one extreme, the subject could learn the unit exactly as it is objectively defined, e.g., DUZ could be learned by forming direct associations between each successive letter in the unit. Alternative methods might involve learning the sound of the unit if it is pronounceable, noting the similarity of the trigram to a meaningful word (in this case, DUZ elicits *does* or the name of the soap product), attachment of words for each letter such as *D*own *U*p *Z*igzag, or even rearrangement of the letters if necessary, e.g., ZUD. These and other methods by which the subject transforms the original unit to some form which is somehow easier for the subject to remember are referred to as encoding (Underwood & Keppel, 1963).

By whatever means the subject transforms the original stimulus unit, if the subject is later required to reproduce the original unit, an opposite process of decoding is necessary. It is not uncommon for a subject to encode successfully but later fail to decode back to the original unit.

Underwood and Keppel (1963) studied encoding and decoding processes in the learning of a list of nonsense syllables or trigrams. It was hypothesized that if encoding was utilized some memory loss would occur as a result of the failure to decode successfully. Since the subject is required to reproduce the original items and not the encoded forms in most learning situations, the failure to decode leads to fewer correct responses on recall. These experimenters also predicted that if the requirement for decoding were removed after some learning had occurred so that the subject was then allowed to recall trigrams with their letters in any arrangement, a sharp rise in performance should result. The present study replicates portions of the Underwood and Keppel study. One additional condition not studied by these experimenters is one in which the subject is not originally required to decode but permitted to recall the trigrams with their letters in any sequence. At some later point in learning a switch will be imposed such that decoding becomes necessary. It is predicted that a sharp drop in performance should result under this condition.

METHOD

Subjects

Each experimenter should obtain four subjects, one for each of the four experimental conditions. Devise some unbiased method for assigning one subject to each of the four conditions.

Materials

The list of 10 trigrams from Underwood and Keppel, (1963) will be used: TFA, BSU, UTB, AMD, DNO, MDI, INP, TPO, ETN, DWE. Each of the 10 trigrams can be transformed into two 3-letter words by rearrangement of the letters of the trigram, e.g., UTB may become TUB or BUT. Print the trigrams on separate 3 x 5 cards. You may wish to prepare two sets of cards for convenience in arranging different presentation orders.

Design

One subject will be instructed to recall the trigrams using any arrangement of the letters within each trigram (Group Any). One subject will be required to reproduce the trigrams so that the letters within each trigram are the same as originally presented (Group Same). One subject will be allowed to recall trigrams in any arrangement of the letters for three trials but then be required to give exact recall of the trigrams for three trials (Group Any-Same). One subject will be required to recall exact arrangements of trigrams for three trials and then be allowed to recall trigrams in any arrangement for three trials (Group Same-Any).

Procedure

After seating your subject in a quiet place, read the following general instructions to subjects in all conditions:

I am going to show you a list of 10 trigrams or three-letter units which are not words. Each trigram is on a separate card and will be shown to you for about 2 seconds each. When I finish showing you each of the 10 trigrams, the first study trial will be over. Then we will have the first test trial. On a slip of paper which I will give you, write down as many of the 10 trigrams as you can recall *in any order*. You will have 40 seconds, after which we shall begin the second study trial. We shall continue with alternate study and test trials until I stop. The order in which the 10 trigrams will be presented to you will differ from trial to trial but your task is to recall as many trigrams as you can in any order.

At this point different instructions are given to different subjects depending upon whether they are to give the trigrams with their *letters* in the same arrangement in which they are presented or in any arrangement.

Groups: Same and Same-Any:	Although the arrangement of the three letters in each trigram you will see on each card will not represent any word, as you will notice once we start, a rearrangement of the letters within any of the 10 trigrams forms a word. However, your task requires that on recall you reproduce the trigrams with their three letters in exactly the same arrangement in which I show them to you.
Groups: Any and Any-Same:	Although the arrangement of the three letters in each trigram you will see on each card will not represent any word, as you will notice once we start, a rearrangement of the letters within any of the 10 trigrams forms a word. If it is easier for you to remember the trigrams by forming words out of them, do so, since your task is to recall the three letters of each trigram in any arrangement.

The above instructions are sufficient for the two conditions in which the subject recalls the trigrams in the same fashion for each of the six trials (Group Any and Group Same). However, additional instructions are necessary for the conditions in which the task of the subject is switched after the third trial. For Group Same-Any, subjects read the following statement *after* Test Trial 3 and *before* Study Trial 4:

On all trials from this point, you may recall the letters within each trigram in *any* order or arrangement which you find easier to recall.

For Group Any-Same subjects, read the following statement *after* Test Trial 3 and before Study Trial 4:

> On all trials from this point, you must recall the letters within each trigram in exactly the same arrangement in which I present them on the cards.

Administer six alternate study and test trials to all subjects in the manner described above. Use a different serial order of list presentation on each trial for each subject. Orders of presentation should be worked out ahead of time. The cards can be re-ordered during each test trial for the following study trial.

Analysis of data

Determine the number of correct responses for each trial as well as the overall trial totals for each of the four conditions. Be sure and change your criterion of scoring after Test Trial 3 in the two conditions involving changed instructions. Combine your data with those of the class. Prepare a graph to illustrate the mean number correct on each trial for each condition.

Compare the mean total correct for Group Same and Group Any using a *t* test for independent data. This comparison permits a determination of the possible benefits of encoding on retention. It is predicted that higher performance will occur in Group Any which does not need to decode but may encode.

Compare the mean total correct on Trials 1 to 3 between Group Same and Group Same-Any. Aside from sampling error, one would not expect any differences in retention since conditions are identical on Trials 1 to 3. Then, compare these two groups on Trials 4 to 6 where Group Same-Any is allowed to encode without decoding required. Does the performance of this group exceed that of Group Same on Trials 4 to 6? Compare it with the level attained on Trials 4 to 6 by Group Any. Compute *t* tests for independent observations for each of these comparisons.

Compare the mean total correct on Trials 1 to 3 between Group Any and Group Any-Same. Since these two conditions are receiving the same treatment on these trials no significant differences would be expected. Compare these two groups on Trials 4 to 6. Is the performance of Group Any-Same lower than that of Group Any? Compare the performance of Group Any-Same with that attained by Group Same on Trials 4 to 6. Use *t* tests for independent observations to determine the significance of obtained differences.

DISCUSSION

1. What evidence is there that most of the subjects in any given condition actually encoded? Although encoding is encouraged when recall is allowed with letters of trigrams in any order, some subjects may refuse to encode and learn the items exactly as presented. Check to see how many subjects on "Any" trials actually recall items in arrangements different from the arrangement presented.

2. In Group Same-Any, did subjects tend to take advantage of the switch in instructions by recalling items in arrangements different from the arrangement presented, or did they continue recalling items in the same arrangements as before the switch?

3. In Group Any-Same, determine whether most subjects actually encoded without decoding by noting if they recalled items in arrangements different from the arrangements in which they were presented on Trials 1 to 3. If they did not recall items in rearranged orders on Trials 1 to 3, then the switch in instructions to require recall in the arrangements presented would not really constitute a switch.

4. Mention situations where you make use of encoding techniques in everyday life.

5. Discuss the relationship between encoding and "rote" learning. In what sense can one argue that no learning is actually "rote"?

REFERENCES

Underwood, B. J., & Keppel, G. Coding processes in verbal learning. *Journal of Verbal Learning and Verbal Behavior,* 1963, **1,** 250–257.

SELECTED BIBLIOGRAPHY

Miller, G. A. *Language and communications.* New York: McGraw-Hill, 1951.

Miller, G. A., Galanter, E., & Pribram, K. *Plans and structure of behavior.* New York: Holt, Rinehart, and Winston, 1960.

Mueller, M. R., Edmonds, E. M., & Evans, S. H. Amount of uncertainty associated with decoding in free recall. *Journal of Experimental Psychology,* 1967, **75**, 437–443.

Underwood, B. J., & Erlebacher, A. H. Studies of coding in verbal behavior. *Psychological Monographs,* 1965, **79**, (13, Whole No. 606).

10 B
EXPERIMENT
UNCERTAINTY OF
DECODING AND RECALL

Although encoding material into forms that facilitate retention can aid memory, it is also likely that interference will occur when the material has to be decoded back into its original form. Thus, in the Underwood and Keppel (1963) study, if UTB is recoded in the more meaningful form BUT, and it is necessary for the subject to recall the original trigram, he may experience difficulty since there are five different decodings for BUT, only one of which is the correct one, UTB.

Mueller, Edmonds, and Evans (1967) as well as Underwood and Erlebacher (1965) have examined the influence of the difficulty of decoding on accuracy of recall. In the Mueller et al. study, subjects learned lists of trigrams that could be encoded as words, for example, AWR into WAR. Some subjects were told that all of the trigrams in their lists were arranged so that the vowel was always either first or last. Given that they could recall the encoded form, WAR, they "knew" that the original trigram had to be AWR or ARW, or WRA or RWA. They could rule out RAW and WAR. There was less uncertainty for this group than for one which received trigrams that were created without any systematic basis. Higher recall of the original trigrams was obtained in the group that received the set of trigrams with less uncertainty.

An extension experiment based on Experiment 10A might involve the replication of the Mueller et al. (1967) study of the effects of decoding uncertainty on recall.

REFERENCES

Mueller, M. R., Edmonds, E. M., & Evans, S. H. Amount of uncertainty associated with decoding in free recall. *Journal of Experimental Psychology,* 1967, **75**, 436–443.

Underwood, B. J., & Erlebacher, A. H., Studies of coding in verbal behavior. *Psychological Monographs,* 1965, **79,** (13, Whole No. 606).

Underwood, B. J., & Keppel, G. Coding processes in verbal learning. *Journal of Verbal Learning and Verbal Behavior,* 1963, **1,** 250–257.

DATA SUMMARY ON CODING: NUMBERS OF CORRECT RECALLS

		Group Any-Order								Group Same-Order					
		Trial								Trial					
	1	2	3	4	5	6	Σ		1	2	3	4	5	6	Σ
S 1								*S* 1							
2								2							
3								3							
4								4							
5								5							
Sn								*Sn*							
M								M							
SD								SD							

DATA SUMMARY ON CODING: NUMBER OF CORRECT RECALLS (CONTINUED)

Group Any-Same Order								Group Same-Any Order							
Trial								Trial							
	1	2	3	4	5	6	Σ		1	2	3	4	5	6	Σ
S 1								S 1							
2								2							
3								3							
4								4							
5								5							
Sn								Sn							

M   M

SD   SD

11 A
EXPERIMENT
FAMILIARITY: DOES IT BREED CONTEMPT OR COMFORT?

Preference and liking seem to be positively correlated with the frequency with which we are exposed to a variety of experiences such as other persons, advertised products, social fads, and words. Although positive correlations between preference and frequency of exposure are plentiful, how are they to be explained? Suppose we do like the people with whom we associate more frequently. Does the mere frequency of contact cause the more favorable evaluations of our frequent associates, or is it our greater liking for certain people in the first place that leads us to increase our frequency of contact with them?

Zajonc (1968) has provided an extensive discussion of the effects of mere exposure on liking and has conducted several experiments in an attempt to support his hypothesis that greater exposure is the antecedent of positive preferences. In a series of studies, he showed the subjects a variety of different materials such as Turkish-like words, Chinese ideographs, and photographs of male faces, varying the frequency of exposure for different stimuli within a given set. The results of his several studies demonstrated that the higher the frequency of exposure, the more positive the evaluations. Contrary to the familiar adage, Zajonc (1970) concluded that familiarity breeds comfort.

Although the effects of contact among members of different ethnic groups are complex (Amir, 1969), one implication of this research is that prejudice and racial strife might be alleviated through increased interracial contact (e.g., Cook, 1969; and Deutsch & Collins, 1951). Zajonc (1970) suggested that mere exposure might even influence the election of political candidates. In view of the possible generality of the exposure effect, it would be interesting to replicate some aspects of Zajonc's (1968) series of studies. In the present study we will compare the evaluative ratings of Turkish-like adjectives as a function of four different frequencies of exposure, 0, 2, 10, 25, using a within-subjects design. Thus, each of your four subjects will receive different stimuli at each of the four different frequencies so that the effects of repeated exposure can be observed for each word at each different frequency. The adjectives will be separated into sets of three words and counterbalanced against the four frequencies of exposure as shown in Table 11.1.

METHOD

Subjects

Each student should obtain four subjects and assign one subject to each of the four counterbalanced arrangements of the four frequency exposures by some randomization procedure.

Materials

Two groupings of Turkish-like words (from Zajonc, 1968) are presented in Table 11.1 and will serve as stimulus words. The two groupings are incorporated so that the verbal context of each word is not always the same for all subjects. Half of the experimenters can use grouping A and the other half can use grouping B.

Table 11.1 also indicates which three words should be shown at each of the four different frequencies. Note that there are four different counterbalanced arrangements so that each subset of words occurs at different frequencies for different subjects.

Procedure

Print each of the 12 words in your grouping (A or B) in the center of a 3 x 5 card. There will be a total of 111 trials for each subject, three words each at the different frequencies of 0, 2, 10, and 25. Each experimenter should prepare a different randomly generated order of presentation of the words for each subject, being sure that the same word does not occur in two consecutive positions. It will be left to you as a class to agree on the "correct" pronunciations of the words beforehand. In order to insure consistent pronunciation, the syllabic form and stressed syllable for each word can be written in light pencil on the back of each card.

Read the following instructions to each subject:

This experiment involves learning how to pronounce foreign words. I will show you a set of foreign words, one on each card. Each time I show you a card, I will pronounce the word correctly and you are to repeat it immediately. The cards contain several presentations of each word, so we will go through the set a number of times until I tell you to stop.

After reading the instructions to your subject, proceed through the series at a 2-second presentation rate. Then read the following instructions:

Actually you have been pronouncing Turkish adjectives. Now I want you to guess their meanings. Of course, it would be unrealistic to expect you to know their exact meanings, so instead I want you to guess their general meanings on a goodness-to-badness scale as to whether you think each word refers to something good or bad.

Hand a copy of Figure 1 to the subject and continue with the instructions:

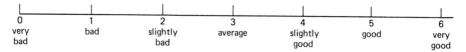

0	1	2	3	4	5	6
very bad	bad	slightly bad	average	slightly good	good	very good

Here is the scale. The numbers range from zero, which indicates very bad, to six, which indicates very good. As I read through each of the 12 words, please tell me the appropriate number on the scale to indicate what you think the word means. You may take as long as you wish to rate each word.

Be sure that you have each subject rate all 12 words, including the three words which each subject did not receive (0 frequency subset). Present and pronounce the stimulus words in orders which insure that no two words from the same frequency subset appear in consecutive positions. Allow each subject to proceed at his own pace and use the columns in Table 11.1 to record your subjects' ratings.

Analysis of data

Combine the ratings for all stimulus words presented with the same frequency of exposure across all subjects. Compute the mean ratings and standard deviations for each of the four presentation frequencies and prepare a figure which demonstrates graphically the favorable-unfavorable rating as a function of successive increments of frequency of exposure.

Compute a mixed-design analysis of variance with repeated measures on frequency of exposure as the dependent-measures dimension. From this analysis you can determine whether there are significant differences among subjects as a function of (a) order of presentation and/or (b) A or B presentation groupings, and within subjects as a function of frequency of exposure.

DISCUSSION

1. Did your study support the finding of Zajonc (1970) that liking is positively correlated with frequency of exposure?

2. Do you think that the effect, if any, was due merely to frequency of exposure? Do you think that the additions of pronouncing the words after the experimenter may have been a critical factor? Why or why not?

3. Can you think of everyday examples that might illustrate the influence of mere exposure on preference and liking?

4. Can you think of situations where increased frequency of contact might actually decrease liking? If so, can these exceptions be reconciled with Zajonc's conclusions?

5. Maddi (1968) suggested that even higher levels of exposure than those used by Zajonc might lead to an eventual decreased liking. What do you think?

6. Jakobovits (1968) noted that the zero exposure frequency words for Zajonc's subjects were rated slightly on the negative side and he suggested that subsequent exposure might only reduce "badness" of stimuli which are initially negatively-valued, but may not increase liking of stimuli which are initially of positive value. Do you think this is a worthwhile distinction and one that can be tested?

REFERENCES

Amir, Y. Contact hypothesis in ethnic relations. *Psychological Bulletin,* 1969, **71**, 319–342.

Cook, S. W. Motives in a conceptual analysis of attitude-related behavior. In W. J. Arnold & D. Levine (Eds.), *Nebraska Symposium on Motivation* (Vol. 17). Lincoln: University of Nebraska Press, 1969.

Deutsch, M., & Collins, M. E. *Interracial housing: A psychological evaluation of a social experiment.* Minneapolis: University of Minnesota Press, 1951.

Jakobovits, L. A. Effects of mere exposure: A comment. *Journal of Personality and Social Psychology Monograph,* 1968, **9**, (2, Pt.2), 30–32.

Maddi, S. R. Meaning, novelty, and affect: Comments on Zajonc's paper. *Journal of Personality and Social Psychology Monograph,* 1968, **9**, (2, Pt. 2), 28–29.

Zajonc, R. B. Attitudinal effects of mere exposure. *Journal of Personality and Social Psychology Monograph,* 1968, **9**, (2, Pt. 2), 1–27.

Zajonc, R. B. Brainwash: Familiarity breed comfort. *Psychology Today,* February pp. 33–35, 60–62.

SELECTED BIBLIOGRAPHY

Amster, H. Semantic satiation and generation: Learning? Adaptation? *Psychological Bulletin,* 1964, **62**, 273–286.

Johnson, R. C., Thomson, C. W., & Frincke, G. Word values, word frequency, and visual duration thresholds. *Psychological Review,* 1960, **67**, 332–342.

Lambert, W. E., & Jakobovits, L. A. Verbal satiation and changes in the intensity of meaning. *Journal of Experimental Psychology,* 1960, **60**, 376–383.

TABLE 11.1:   STIMULUS WORDS COUNTERBALANCED AGAINST FOUR
              FREQUENCY EXPOSURE PRESENTATIONS AND
              SUBJECT RATING RECORD SHEET*

Stimulus Words Groupings		Exposure Frequencies			
A	B	S_1 Ratings	S_2 Ratings	S_3 Ratings	S_4 Ratings
IKTITAF	AFWORBU	0	2	10	25
BIWOJNI	SARICIK	0	2	10	25
ZABULON	ENANWAL	0	2	10	25
AFWORBU	IKTITAF	2	25	0	10
NANSOMA	CIVDRA	2	25	0	10
LOKANTA	JANDARA	2	25	0	10
SARICIK	LOKANTA	10	0	25	2
KADIRGA	BIWOJNI	10	0	25	2
JANDARA	DILIKLI	10	0	25	2
ENANWAL	KADIRGA	25	10	2	0
DILIKLI	ZABULON	25	10	2	0
CIVDRA	NANSOMA	25	10	2	0

*Adapted from Zajonc, 1968

11 B
EXPERIMENT
DOES MERE EXPOSURE ALWAYS LEAD TO GREATER LIKING?

Zajonc (1970) and Zajonc, Swap, Harrison and Roberts (1971) recognized that there are situations where increased exposure may lead to a reduction in liking rather than an increase as Zajonc had found earlier (Zajonc, 1968). One factor that is critical is the initial value of the stimulus. If it is of neutral value, then increased exposure may enhance liking; however, for stimuli of initial negative value, it is possible that increased exposure may increase dislike.

Ordinarily persons avoid stimuli that they dislike if they have a choice. This behavior contributes to the apparent positive correlation between frequency of voluntary contact and liking. On the other hand, if the exposure to stimuli is beyond the control of the subject, so that the negatively-valued stimuli cannot be readily avoided by the subject, Zajonc's (1968) generalization may break down for negatively-valued stimuli.

Several recent studies confirm these conjectures (Brickman, Redfield, Harrison, & Crandall, 1972; Burgess & Sales, 1971; and Perlman & Oskamp, 1971).

For example, Burgess and Sales (1971) asked the subjects to memorize pairs of nonsense syllables and words that were shown with varying frequencies. The words varied in affective tone, being positive, negative, or neutral in meaning. After studying the pairs, the subjects were instructed to rate the likeability of the nonsense syllables. The results showed that nonsense syllables that had been paired with positive words were more liked the more frequently they had been seen, but that the opposite was true with nonsense syllables that had been paired with negative words. Frequency of exposure had no bearing on liking for nonsense syllables paired with neutral words.

In another study, Perlman and Oskamp (1971) had the subjects rate photographs of a black or white male in one of three contexts, positive (clergyman's attire), negative (prison garb), or neutral (street clothes). Regardless of the model, increased liking occurred with increased exposure for the positive context while increased disliking occurred with greater exposure for the negative context. Again, the neutral context did not show a frequency effect.

When Spiro Agnew had moved from an unknown name to become a household word, Zajonc (1970) indicated that after repeated exposure, the attitude toward almost anything becomes more favorable, "even Spiro Agnew" (p. 60). After Agnew fell into disrepute in 1973, one would expect that repeated exposure should have a different effect from that prior to 1970.

A logical extension of Experiment 11A would be to replicate the Zajonc methodlogy using stimuli which are somewhat negative in initial value.

REFERENCES

Brickman, P., Redfield, J., Harrison, A. A., & Crandall, R. Drive and predisposition as factors in the attitudinal effects of mere exposure. *Journal of Experimental and Social Psychology,* 1972, **8,** 31–44.

Burgess, T. D. G., Jr., & Sales, S. M. Attitudinal effects of mere exposure: A re-evaluation. *Journal of Experimental and Social Psychology,* 1971, **7,** 461–472.

Perlman, D., & Oskamp, S. The effects of picture content and exposure frequency on evaluations of Negroes and whites. *Journal of Experimental and Social Psychology,* 1971, **7,** 503–514.

Zajonc, R. B. Attitudinal effects of mere exposure. *Journal of Personality and Social Psychology Monograph,* 1968, **9,** (2, pt. 2), 1–27.

Zajonc, R. B. Brainwash; Familarity breeds comfort. *Psychology Today,* February, 1970, pp. 33–35; 60–62.

Zajonc, R. B., Swap, W. C., Harrison, A. A., & Roberts, P. Limiting conditions of the exposure effect: Satiation and relativity. *Journal of Personality and Social Psychology,* 1971, **18,** 384–391.

DATA SUMMARY ON EFFECTS OF FREQUENCY OF EXPOSURE: MEAN RATING FOR THREE WORDS AT EACH FREQUENCY

	Frequency of Exposure			
	0	2	10	25
S 1				
2				
3				
4				
5				
S_n				
	M SD	M SD	M SD	M SD

12 A
EXPERIMENT
IDENTIFICATION OF CONJUNCTIVE
AND DISJUNCTIVE CONCEPTS

A concept may be defined as a common attribute of several dissimilar stimuli which elicits the same response. "Table" is a concept which is applicable to a variety of stimulus objects that are commonly identified by their "tableness." Similarly "roundness," "largeness," and so on, are concepts which refer to some attribute specifiable in a number of otherwise dissimilar stimuli.

Psychologists like Bruner, Goodnow, and Austin (1956) have been interested in studying how people form or identify concepts. A display of 81 stimulus cards which contained four different dimensions or attributes was used. Each card varied in (a) type of geometrical form (circle, square, or cross); (b) number of forms (1, 2, or 3); (c) number of borders (1, 2, or 3); and (d) color of forms and borders (green, red, or black). Thus there were three values of each of the four different attributes or stimulus dimensions which produced a deck of 81 different combinations, each instance exhibiting one value of each of the four attributes.

The general procedure in testing a subject was as follows: the subject was informed that the experimenter had a concept in mind and that certain cards in the display would illustrate it while others would not. First, he was shown a card which was a positive instance, that is, it illustrated the concept that the experimenter had in mind. Then the subject selected cards in any order he chose from the display and the experimenter informed him after each choice whether it was a positive or negative instance. After each card selected by the subject, he could choose to offer only one hypothesis regarding the concept. This procedure continued until the subject correctly identified the concept. The use of paper and pencil was not allowed.

Bruner et al. (1956) refer to a concept or a "category" of instances in terms of the defining attributes of some subset of the display. For example, the concept might be all cards with one red form or all cards with one form and/or with a circle. A distinction is made between conjunctive (C) and disjunctive (D) concepts. A conjunctive concept is defined by the *joint presence* of the appropriate value of two or more attributes, for example, all cards containing red circles, that is, redness and circleness occurring together. Disjunctive concepts are of an inclusive either/or [or both] nature, for example, all cards that have red forms or have circles, or both.

Bruner et al. (1956) found that conjunctive concepts were much easier to identify that disjunctive concepts. Similar findings (Conant & Trabasso, 1964) were obtained using problems which were equivalent structurally, perceptually, and informationally. The present experiment, which is based on the Conant and Trabasso (1964) study, will examine conjunctive and disjunctive concept solutions. Although Conant and Trabasso (1964) had all subjects solve both types of problems, this study employs different subjects for the two types of problems, in order to simplify the experimental design and analysis of the results.

METHOD

Subjects

Each experimenter should obtain at least four subjects, two to be assigned to each of the two experimental conditions (C problems and D problems). Devise some unbiased method for assigning two subjects to each of the two conditions.

Materials

The stimuli (see Table 12.1) consist of 16 pairs each of which contains a triangle on the left and a circle on the right. The figures, however, differ in two dimensions: size (large and small) and color (black and white). The 16 pairs represent different combinations of the two values of the two dimensions of the two forms. The stimuli should be cut out and affixed to 3 x 5 cards.

Procedure

At the outset of the experiment, arrange the 16 cards in any unsystematic 4 x 4 display in front of your subject. In general, the experiment is conducted as follows: Explain the nature of the stimuli, describing the dimensions and values. Give appropriate instructions for either conjunctive or disjunctive problems as shown below. In order to be certain that your subject understands the general nature of the relevant concept, have your subject identify all the positive and negative instances associated with a sample concept selected by the experimenter. Then begin a problem by presenting your subject with one of the 16 cards and telling the subject whether it is a positive or negative instance of the unknown concept which the subject is to identify (see Table 12.2). The subject's task is to choose one at a time from the remaining cards the one he thinks will give him the most information about the correct concept. After your subject selects each card, inform him as to whether it is a positive or negative instance. The experimenter should thoroughly familiarize himself with the positive and negative instances of each concept, so that he can give each subject correct information about each choice without undue hesitation. This is the likeliest source of difficulty in this procedure, since the experimenter must be prepared to deal with any of the possible orders of cards selected by each subject for each concept.) Arrange the subject's choices in two separate rows, one for positive instances and one for negative instances of the concept. The subject is allowed to offer only one hypothesis as to what he thinks the concept is after each selection; although premature verbalizations are to be discouraged, he is to continue selecting instances until he can verbalize the correct concept. Do not tell the subject what his previous hypotheses have been even if he should ask.

Read the following instructions to all subjects at the outset:

> Before you on the table are 16 cards each containing a triangle and a circle. The circles and triangles are either large or small and either black or white. In this experiment, we shall define a "concept" as some subset or portion of these 16 cards which have some common attributes. You will be asked to attempt to identify the concept which I have in mind as best you can in a manner which I shall now describe to you.

Below are separate instructions for the conjunctive and disjunctive problems.

Conjunctive. As an example, the concept I might have in mind could be all those cards containing *both* large triangles and white circles. Please point out all cards in the set which contain both large triangles and white circles.

[After the subject identifies the appropriate cards.] That is correct. There are 4 cards illustrating the concept and 12 which do not. This will be true of all the concepts I am going to ask you to identify.

Please note that in the type of concepts we are dealing with, just one property of the circles is required (the size or the color) and one property (the size or the color), not necessarily the same, is required for triangles. That is, small or black triangles is not one of the type of concepts we will use since it concerns two properties of one figure. We shall use only concepts involving one property of the circles and one property of the triangles. Any questions?

Disjunctive. As an example, the concept I might have in mind could be all those cards which contain *either* large triangles *or* white circles *or* both. Please point out all cards in the set which contain either large triangles or white circles or both.

[After the subject identifies the appropriate cards.] That is correct. Twelve of the 16 cards illustrate the concept and four do not. This will be true of all the concepts I am going to ask you to identify.

Please note that in the type of concepts we are dealing with, just one property of circles is required (the size or the color) and one property (the size or the color), not necessarily the same, is required for triangles. That is, small or black triangles is not one of the type of concepts we will use since it concerns two properties of one figure. We shall use only concepts involving one property of the circles *or* one property of the triangles or both. Any questions?

The instructions below are identical for both the conjunctive (C) and disjunctive (D) conditions and are to be read next.

I will give you a card which is *or* is not (and I will tell you which is the case) an example of the concept I want you to identify. You are to try other cards, one at a time. After each choice, I will tell you whether or not it is an example of the concept. You may make one judgment as to what the concept is after each card you select. There is no penalty if you choose cards that are not examples of the concept.

Your score depends on how many cards you need to choose before you correctly identify the concept. The fewer choices you make, the better the score you receive, obviously. When you think you know the concept, inform me, but please avoid premature guessing. If you are correct we will start the next problem. Time is not a factor, only the number of cards you choose. There is no need to rush; take as much time as you need. You may rearrange the cards during the session in any way you think helpful. For your convenience, we will make two rows at the side, one for the cards you choose which are positive examples and one for those which are negative examples of the concept. Any questions?

Record the number of positive instances, the number of negative instances, and the total number of instances selected by each subject for each concept, together with the hypotheses offered by the subject in the course of attaining the correct concept. After the subject has identified all three of the concepts, ask him to describe his techniques or strategies for solving the problems, including a consideration as to whether there were changes from one problem to another.

Problems

The actual problems, together with the initial example to be given to the subject in each case, are shown in Table 12.2 (from Conant & Trabasso, 1964). There are 16 possible combinations of the circle-values and triangle-values, and hence 16 possible solutions. If an example card is positive for a C problem or negative for a D problem, there are 4 positive instances and 12 negative instances of the concept in the set of 16 combinations; hence 12 possible solutions are eliminated. (See the sample concept in the instructions for the conjunctive condition.) Similarly, if an example card is negative for a C problem or positive for a D problem, there are 12 positive instances and 4 negative instances of the concept in the set of 16 combinations; hence 4 possible solutions are eliminated. (See the sample concept in the instructions for the disjunctive condition.) As Conant and Trabasso point out: "Thus, positive C instances and negative D instances yield the most information and their respective selection would lead to the most efficient C or D problem solving. When the example card was positive, a C problem could be solved in two card choices, and a D problem in three or four choices, depending on the subject's first card choice. When the example card was negative, a D problem required two choices and a C problem, three or four. The C and D sets of three problems each were equated as to the minimum number of choices necessary for solution, 8–10 choices. . . ." (Conant & Trabasso, 1964, p. 252).

Analysis of data

For each subject in the C condition, find the average number of cards required to reach criterion. Do the same for each subject in the D condition. Your dependent variable is thus the mean number of cards per subject required to reach the learning criterion. This can be found by averaging the mean scores for the subjects of all experimenters within the C and D conditions respectively. Include the initial example cards in the total count. Compare the means for the two conditions by the use of a t test for independent groups (uncorrelated data). Find and compare the ranges of the mean number of choices per subject required for solution in the two types of problems.

DISCUSSION

1. Which type of problem, conjunctive or disjunctive, required the least number of cards to solve on the average?

2. The subjects may have varied in their performances within each of the conditions. Find the ranges of the mean number of choices per subject within the C condition and within the D condition, respectively, and compare the ranges. Did the difficulty of the problems *within* each set vary as widely as the difference *between* the sets of different type problems?

3. Assuming conjunctive problems were solved faster, how do you account for this superiority? What makes disjunctive problems difficult?

4. If the subject were to select instances throughout a problem at random, the proportion of positive instances chosen should be about .25 for C concepts and about .75 for D concepts. Bruner

et al. (1956) point out that a "positive-focusing strategy" is more efficient for C concepts, and a "negative-focusing strategy" is more efficient for D concepts. If these strategies are used, the proportions of positive choices for C and D concepts should be higher and lower respectively. Did your subjects show evidence of using these strategies?

5. How do subjects report subjectively their "strategies" or techniques for solving the two problem types? Is it the same process for both types? Does their report agree with the impression you formed during your observation of the subject's sequence of choices of cards during the test?

REFERENCES

Bruner, J. S., Goodnow, J. J., & Austin, G. A. *A study of thinking.* New York: Wiley, 1956.

Conant, M. B., & Trabasso, T. Conjunctive and disjunctive concept formation under equal-information conditions. *Journal of Experimental Psychology,* 1964, **67**, 250–255.

SELECTED BIBLIOGRAPHY

Bourne, L. E., Jr. *Human conceptual behavior.* Boston: Allyn-Bacon, 1966.

Hovland, C. I., & Weiss, W. Transmission of information concerning concepts through positive and negative instances. *Journal of Experimental Psychology*, 1953, **45**, 175–182.

Hunt, E. B. *Concept learning: An information processing problem.* New York: Wiley, 1962.

TABLE 12.1: STIMULUS MATERIALS (ADAPTED FROM CONANT & TRABASSO, 1964)

TABLE 12.1 (CONTINUED)

TABLE 12.2: CONJUNCTIVE AND INCLUSIVE DISJUNCTIVE SETS

Problem	Concept Triangle Circle	Example Given to S Triangle	Circle	Instance
C 1	W and L	S, W	L, B	Positive
C 2	L and B	S, W	S, B	Negative
C 3	B and S	L, B	L, W	Negative
D 1	L and/or B	L, W	L, W	Positive
D 2	W and/or W	L, B	S, B	Negative
D 3	S and/or L	S, B	S, W	Positive

Note: The values of the stimuli are W (White), B (Black), L (Large), & S (Small).

From "Conjunctive and Disjunctive Concept Formation under Equal-information conditions" by M. B. Conant and T. Trabasso, *Journal of Experimental Psychology*, 1964, 67, 250–255. Copyright 1964 by the American Psychological Association. Reprinted by permission.

12 B
EXPERIMENT
CONJUNCTIVE VERSUS
DISJUNCTIVE RULE LEARNING

As Haygood and Bourne (1965) have noted, many of the studies of concept learning are actually concerned with attribute identification rather than the learning of concepts or rules. Usually, the experimenter defines the conceptual rule, such as conjunction or disjunction which is embodied in the materials to be received and the subject's task is to identify the relevant attributes for each problem. Rule learning, itself, is not necessary in most of these studies.

The Conant and Trabasso (1964) study was similarly restricted to the analysis of attribute identification. One could modify the study, omitting any explanation about conjunction and disjunction to the subjects, so that their task would be to discover these rules. One would use several problems of each rule type and for each problem present all of the instances in the Conant and Trabasso set of stimuli. The subject would be informed whether each instance was positive or negative. It would probably be essential to place positive and negative instances in two separate display groupings in front of the subject so as to aid him in the discovery of the rule. A number of studies with college students (Haygood & Bourne, 1965; Schaeffer & Wallce, 1968) as well as with children (DiVesta & Walls, 1969) have shown that the disjunctive rule is much more difficult to learn. The extension study is aimed at examining this result with the Conant and Trabasso materials.

REFERENCES

Conant, M. B., & Trabasso, T. Conjunctive and disjunctive concept formation under equal-information conditions. *Journal of Experimental Psychology,* 1964, **67**, 250–255.

DiVesta, F. J., & Walls, R. T. Rule and attribute identification in children's attainment of disjunctive and conjunctive concepts. *Journal of Experimental Psychology,* 1969, **80,** 498–504.

Haygood, R. C., & Bourne, L. E., Jr. Attribute- and rule-learning aspects of conceptual behavior. *Psychological Review,* 1965, **72,** 175–195.

Schaeffer, B., & Wallace, R. Interdependence of rule-learning and attribute learning. *Perceptual and Motor Skills,* 1968, **27,** 239–246.

DATA SUMMARY ON CONCEPT/IDENTIFICATION: NUMBER OF CARDS TO SOLUTION

	Conjunctive											
	Problem No.											
	1			2			3			Σ		
	+	−	Total	+	−	Total	+	−	Total	+	−	Total
S 1												
2												
3												
4												
5												
Sn												
		M			M			M			M	
		SD			SD			SD			SD	

DATA SUMMARY ON CONCEPT/IDENTIFICATION: NUMBER
OF CARDS TO SOLUTION (CONTINUED)

Disjunctive

Problem No.

	1			2			3			Σ		
	+	−	Total	+	−	Total	+	−	Total	+	−	Total
S 1												
2												
3												
4												
5												
Sn												

M   M   M   M

SD   SD   SD   SD

13 A
EXPERIMENT
CATEGORY SET
IN ANAGRAM SOLUTIONS

Deese (1959) has found that an important factor in free recall of verbal materials is the inter-item associative strength (IIAS) within the list to be recalled. IIAS is a measure of the interrelationships among units of a list. High IIAS exists if the units comprising a list tend to evoke each other frequently as associates, whereas IIAS is low if the units of the list seldom elicit one another as associates. When the items within a list are highly interassociated, free recall is enhanced. The recall of a given word tends to increase total recall by eliciting other related words in the list of high IIAS.

Some investigators (Mayzner & Tresselt, 1958; Safren, 1962) see a similarity between such verbal behavior situations and anagram solution and expect similar principles to operate in both situations. Safren (1962) attempted to exhibit this similarity by showing that a "category set" exists in anagram solution as well as in verbal recall (Deese, 1959). A category set may be viewed as a readiness to respond to words belonging to a common class or category, i.e., a group of words with high inter-item associative connections. Thus, a list of anagrams whose solutions belong to a common category might be expected to be solved more readily than a list composed of unrelated word solutions. For example, all of the solutions to the anagrams in List 4 (Table 13.1) are related to "beverages," "breakfast," "food," and "taste." If a category set comes into operation during the course of solving a list, the solution time for the anagrams should be shorter than that for a control group which receives a list of equal length, but made up of unrelated words. Moreover, there should be a decrease in solution time for successive anagrams when subjects solve anagrams made from associatively related words since associations called up by previously solved anagrams will aid the subject in the solution of later problems in the list.

The subjects in one group in Safren's experiment received one of six different lists of six anagrams each. All word solutions (words from which anagrams were made) within any given list were highly interrelated.

The control group subjects received one of 36 different lists of six anagrams each. However the word solutions within each of these lists were unrelated.

The results of Safren's experiment supported the two main predictions: (a) that time for solution would be shorter for anagrams from organized lists where anagrams belonged to a common category, and (b) that the group with the organized lists would show a greater decrease in solution time over successive anagrams in the list. A third group, which will not be repeated in this experiment, received category labels in addition to the organized lists. This group had the shortest solution times but did not show improvement over problems, presumably because the category label that was supplied evoked some of the anagram solutions from the outset.

This study is a partial replication of Safren's experiment. A comparison of solution times and improvement within a given list of six anagrams will be made between the two types of lists, organized and unrelated.

METHOD

Subjects

Each experimenter will obtain two subjects of similar age and education. Assign the first subject to one of the two conditions by the toss of a coin. The second subject will be assigned to the other condition.

Materials

Table 13.1 contains a total of 36 anagrams arranged in six lists of six anagrams each. The arrangements are such that the solutions in each list form a common category, e.g., List 1 solutions are words related to "military." Safren constructed these lists by giving word association tests to a separate group of subjects to determine empirically that the words of each list are interassociated.

From these organized lists, different lists of six unrelated words can be obtained by taking one word from each of the six organized lists for each unrelated list. It is possible to form 36 different unrelated lists of six words with each word appearing six times as Safren did, but it will be sufficient for this experiment to use one unrelated list. Construct your list by using all words in any given row of Table 13.1 (across categories) as the unrelated list. Prepare the items to be presented to your subjects by cutting out the anagrams in Table 13.1 and fastening each one to a card, or by printing each anagram on a small   card.

Details of the rules for generating the particular rearrangements of each word into an anagram are given in Safren (1962) and will not be repeated here. Only one solution is possible for all but two of Safren's words. She reported that no subject offered any but the solutions shown in Table 13.1.

Procedure

After your subject is seated comfortably in a quiet place, read the following instructions:

This is an experiment on anagram solution. As you may know, an anagram is a word with its letters rearranged. I will show you a number of anagrams, one at a time. You are to determine without the aid of paper and pencil what the original word is. Work as rapidly as you can since you will be allowed a maximum of 4 minutes for each anagram. As soon as you have a solution, tell me what it is. If you cannot solve any anagram in the time allotted, we will stop and go to the next one after I give you the answer. You will solve six different anagrams. Have you any questions? (Pause.) Here is the first anagram.

After each anagram is completed, announce to your subject:

Here is the next anagram.

Use the list of six anagrams from any one row in Table 13.1 for the unrelated list and use the list of six anagrams from any one column in Table 13.1 for the organized list. Ideally the six anagrams within a list should be presented in all possible serial orders for different subjects. That is, within a given list, the first word should not always be first, but should appear equally as often in all ordinal positions for different subjects. This arrangement would balance out practice effects and any possible differences in difficulty level in going from word to word. However, for the purposes of this experiment, it will suffice if each experimenter uses a different order of the words within the lists for his subjects. This ordering should be randomized by thorough shuffling of the cards.

Record the time in seconds for the solution of each anagram. If your subject fails to solve any anagram within 4 minutes, stop him and record 240 seconds as his solution time. Give your subject the solution and then present the next anagram. As you go through the list, present the next anagram as soon as you have recorded the solution time for the

TABLE 13.1: SIX ORGANIZED LISTS OF ANAGRAMS*
(Solutions in Parentheses)

List 1		List 2		List 3		List 4		List 5		List 6	
CANDOMM	(COMMAND)	WHELIST	(WHISTLE)	RIACH	(CHAIR)	LIMK	(MILK)	DOROCT	(DOCTOR)	SAQURE	(SQUARE)
REDOR	(ORDER)	TARNI	(TRAIN)	FOST	(SOFT)	RECAM	(CREAM)	URNSE	(NURSE)	CIRLEC	(CIRCLE)
RAMY	(ARMY)	NESOI	(NOISE)	OFAS	(SOFA)	USGRA	(SUGAR)	EHALHT	(HEALTH)	DUNRO	(ROUND)
OYEB	(OBEY)	UNDOS	(SOUND)	CUNSHIO	(CUSHION)	EFECOF	(COFFEE)	KISC	(SICK)	BECU	(CUBE)
SODLERI	(SOLDIER)	SHLIRL	(SHRILL)	WOLPIL	(PILLOW)	SEWTE	(SWEET)	MEDCIENI	(MEDICINE)	CLOBK	(BLOCK)
VANY	(NAVY)	OLDU	(LOUD)	COCHU	(COUCH)	DINRK	(DRINK)	ECRU	(CURE)	LALB	(BALL)

*Adapted from Safren, 1962.

preceding one. Do not discuss the experiment with your subject until all six anagrams have been presented.

Analysis of data

Combine the solution times you have recorded with those of the remainder of the class for each anagram on the lists for the two conditions. Compute the *median* solution times for anagrams 1 through 6 for the two conditions separately. Analyze the anagrams in their order of presentation for the subjects even though different subjects will have had different problems in each of these positions. Prepare a graph showing any changes in solution times over successive problems for each of the two conditions.

Determine whether there is a statistically significant difference between median solution times on the list for the organized and unrelated conditions by applying the Mann-Whitney U test.

DISCUSSION

1. What changes in solution times appeared over the six succesive anagrams for the organized list group? For the unrelated list group?

2. Were the unrelated and organized list groups approximately equal in solution time for each anagram at the outset of the experiment? At the end? Were any differences that you observed in the expected direction?

3. Is it conceivable that the formation of a category set might actually impede rather than facilitate solution time? How? Can you suggest an experimental design to test the hypothesis that anagram solution might be impeded with the formation of a category set?

REFERENCES

Deese, J. Influence of inter-item associative strength upon immediate recall. *Psychological Reports,* 1959, **5**, 305–312.

Mayzner, M. S., & Tresselt, M. E. Anagram solution times: A function of letter order and word frequency. *Journal of Experimental Psychology,* 1958, **56**, 376–379.

Safren, Miriam A. Associations, sets, and the solution of word problems. *Journal of Experimental Psychology,* 1962, **64**, 40–45.

SELECTED BIBLIOGRAPHY

Maltzman, I., & Morrisett, L., Jr. Different strengths of set in the solution of anagrams. *Journal of Experimental Psychology,* 1952, **44**, 242–246.

Reese, H. J. & Israel, H. E. Investigation of the establishment and operation of mental sets. *Psychological Monographs,* 1935, **46**, No. 6 (Whole No. 210).

Siegel, S., *Nonparametric statistics for the behavioral sciences.* New York: McGraw-Hill, 1956.

13 B
EXPERIMENT
DIRECT AND ASSOCIATIVE PRIMING OF ANAGRAM SOLUTIONS

The procedure of associative priming is closely related to Safren's (1962) concept of category set and has been used by Maltzman and Morrisett (1952) and Dominowski and Ekstrand (1967) as a means of facilitating problem solving. In the latter study, three types of priming given to subjects before receiving a list of 10 anagrams to solve were compared. One group (direct priming) was shown a list of the actual solution words and told that they were seeing the answers. A second group (associative priming) was more akin to Safren's (1962) experimental condition. These subjects were shown a list of words which were associatively related to the anagram solutions. A third group was led to believe that the list they saw before attempting the anagrams was related, but in actual fact, the words they saw were not appropriate solutions. A fourth group, which served as the control, did not receive any type of priming list. Results indicated significantly faster solution times for the two priming conditions, direct and associative priming.

These results from the Dominowski and Ekstrand study illustrate the influence of associative processes on cognition. As in Safren's experiment, the activation of associative connections leading to the problem solution led to faster performance. An interesting followup to the Safren study would be to replicate the Dominowski and Ekstrand (1967) study using the stimulus materials developed by them.

REFERENCES

Dominowski, R. L., & Ekstrand, B. R. Direct and associative priming in anagram solving. *Journal of Experimental Psychology,* 1967, **74,** 84–86.

Maltzman, I., & Morrisett, L. Different strengths of set in the solution of anagrams. *Journal of Experimental Psychology,* 1952, **44,** 242–246.

Safren, M. A. Associations, set, and the solution of word problems. *Journal of Experimental Psychology,* 1962, **64,** 40—45.

DATA SUMMARY ON CATEGORY SET: SOLUTION TIMES

Unrelated List								Organized List						
Anagram								Anagram						
	1st	2nd	3rd	4th	5th	6th			1st	2nd	3rd	4th	5th	6th
S 1								*S* 1						
2								2						
3								3						
4								4						
5								5						
Sn								*Sn*						

Median
Time
per
Ana-
gram

Median
Time
per
Ana-
gram

14 A
EXPERIMENT
RISK TAKING AS A FUNCTION
OF RANGE OF PAYOFFS

Whether or not we take risks or decide to gamble depends on numerous complex factors. Disregarding the totally reckless, most of us would probably ask ourselves the general question, is the risk worth taking? For example, suppose you are a healthy person and you are offered some vitamins of unproven quality. It is claimed that these pills will give you lots of pep, but it is possible that they may be injurious. The risk, in view of your current good health, is not worth taking. On the other hand suppose you are on your deathbed and some pills are offered that are guaranteed to restore you to an active life. Of course, they may also speed you on your way. Despite this unpleasant possibility, the risk here is more attractive. Thus, whether or not a person is willing to gamble, and hence win or lose, depends in large measure on his current state of health, wealth, or whatever he is risking.

Myers and Sadler (1960) devised a situation to study risk-taking behavior in which subjects could "win or lose" varying amounts of money on each of a series of trials. First, the subject was required to draw a card from a deck. A monetary outcome was printed on each card. This deck of cards contained 50 gains and 50 losses (+ and − values) of the same magnitude. An element of risk was introduced by then allowing the subject the choice of accepting the outcome from this deck on each trial or of gambling, that is, taking the risk that the outcome from a second deck might be more favorable. If the subject, after considering the Deck 1 outcome, elected to risk the Deck 2 outcome, he was obliged to accept the outcome of the second deck. Even if the subject chose not to gamble on a particular trial after viewing the Deck 1 outcome, he was always shown the Deck 2 outcome, the outcome he would have received had he decided to gamble. Trials consisting of fixed Deck 1 outcomes and the choice of whether or not to gamble on Deck 2 were continued until the two decks of 100 cards each were completed.

Myers and Sadler (1960) studied risk taking in this task as a function of the range of payoffs in Deck 2. The average payoff in the decks they used was zero but the range of payoffs varied. They found that when the Deck 1 outcome was a gain, the greater the Deck 2 range of payoff, the more the subject tended to gamble. On the other hand, large ranges of payoffs on Deck 2 led to less gambling on trials in which losses occurred in Deck 1.

The present study, which is based on the Myers and Sadler (1960) study, will also examine the effects of the range of payoffs in Deck 2 on risk-taking behavior.

METHOD

Subjects

Each experimenter should obtain two subjects, one for each condition. Try to select your subjects from the same age range. Devise some unbiased method for assigning one subject to each of the two conditions.

Materials

Prepare three decks of 100 cards each. In Deck 1, there should be 50 cards marked +$1 and 50 cards marked -$1. Deck 2A (small range) should consist of 10 cards with each of the following values: -$6, -$5, -$4, -$3, -$2, +$2, +$3, +$4, +$5, and +$6. In Deck 2B (large range) each value between -$11 and +$11 should be represented five times each with the exception of -$1, $0, and +$1. The values -$1, $0, and +$1 are not used in Decks 2A and 2B in order to insure that S will have either a net gain or a net loss relative to Deck 1 in every trial on which the subject gambles.

Several experimenters may be able to collaborate in preparing the necessary decks of cards and share the stimulus materials for this experiment.

Procedure

The general procedure is as follows. Deck 1 will serve as the first deck for both experimental conditions. The subject in one condition will receive Deck 2A as the second deck, and the subject in the other condition will receive Deck 2B as the second deck. Deck 1 and the appropriate second deck are placed face down in front of the subject with Deck 1 on his left. First, the subject takes the top card from Deck 1. This card constitutes the fixed payoff. Having examined this payoff, the subject must decide to accept or reject it. If he decides to accept it, he gains or loses $1 according to what is marked on the card. If the subject decides to reject the Deck 1 outcome, i.e., gamble, he is to turn over the top card from the second deck. He must then accept that outcome for better or for worse, and his gain or loss will be the amount shown on the Deck 2 card. Even though he decides not to gamble, i.e., to accept the Deck 1 outcome, the subject is required to see what he would have received had he chosen from his second deck.

Number a sheet of paper from 1 to 100, allowing two columns opposite each number. The first column will be used to record the outcome of Deck 1. Record this outcome *regardless* of the subject's decision with respect to gambling. If he does gamble, i.e., decide to select the card from his second deck, *draw a circle around the Deck 1 outcome to indicate that he did not accept that Deck 1 outcome.* In the second column, record the outcome which occurs on his second deck, regardless of whether or not the subject gambled on that trial.

Note that the optimal strategy for maximizing the gains in a task such as this, where the mean outcome is 0, is to accept all the +$1's from Deck 1 and to gamble on all outcomes of -$1 from Deck 1. This applies to both experimental conditions since the range of the outcomes is *not* a factor with respect to net gain or loss. However, psychologically, ranges of different magnitudes may differentially affect the subject's behavior, and that is one question to be answered in this study.

The following instructions are to be read to each subject after you have seated him in a quiet place free from distractions.

> Before you are two decks of cards. On each trial, you are to remove the top card from the deck on your left (Deck 1) and examine its outcome. You may decide to accept or reject that card and its outcome. If you accept on a given trial, that is, prefer not to gamble, simply state your decision. So that you can know what would have happened had you decided to gamble, I will always show you the outcome you would have received from the second deck. Then we will start the next trial. However, if you decide to reject the outcome from the first deck and prefer to gamble on the card in the second deck having a more favorable outcome, state your decision and then remove the top card from the deck on your right (Deck 2). You must then accept that outcome, be it better or worse than that you obtained from the first deck. Deck 1 contains only +$1 and -$1 outcomes, whereas the second deck contains

plus and minus outcomes greater than $1. Your goal, naturally, is to try to win as much as possible from the two decks of cards.

Then shuffle each deck and have the subject begin the task. When the subject has completed the 100 trials ask him to estimate the average value of the outcomes in his second deck. Ask the subject to describe the strategy employed during the task. Determine the net gain or loss for the subject.

Analysis of data

For both subjects, small and large range, divide the 100 trials into four blocks of 25 trials each. Within each of the four blocks of 25 trials, determine the percentage of trials on which "gambling" occurred *separately* for those trials on which Deck 1 led to +$1 and for those trials on which Deck 1 yielded a -$1 outcome. Combine the data of your subjects with those of other experimenters. Plot a graph showing these percentages on +$1 and -$1 Deck 1 outcomes for both groups over the four blocks of trials.

Use a *t* test for correlated data to compare the overall (100 trials) percentage of gambling for each group for the two types of Deck 1 outcomes. Are the percentages significantly different?

DISCUSSION

1. Did more gambling occur on +$1 or -$1 Deck 1 outcomes? Was this observed in both groups?

2. Were there any differences in amount of gambling between the large-range amd small-range groups? On all trials? On trials with +$1 Deck 1 outcomes? On trials with -$1 Deck 1 outcomes?

3. What appears to be the strategy most commonly employed by subjects? Which strategy appeared to be most successful in terms of maximizing gains under these experimental conditions? Did subjects with different strategies give different estimates of the average value of the outcomes in their second decks? Were there any consistent differences in the estimates of the average value of the second decks by subjects with net gains and subjects with net losses?

4. In describing the risk-taking studies of Myers and his associates in a review article addressed to the question of sources of variation in risk-taking behavior, Slovic (1964) commented that "unfortunately, no data on individual differences were reported." Did you find substantial individual differences between subjects within each group?

5. Do you think that decks containing different distributions of outcomes from those employed in this experiment would lead to different results? Describe several variations that might be used, and in each case predict how the results might vary from those in the present study.

REFERENCES

Myers, J. L., & Sadler, E. Effects of range of payoffs as a variable in risk taking. *Journal of Experimental Psychology,* 1960, **60,** 306–309.

Slovic, P. Assessment of risk taking behavior. *Psychology Bulletin,* 1964, **61,** 220–233.

SELECTED BIBLIOGRAPHY

Katz, L. Monetary incentive and range of payoffs as determiners of risk taking. *Journal of Experimental Psychology,* 1962, **64,** 541–544.

Myers, J. L., & Katz, L. Range of payoffs and feedback in risk taking. *Psychological Reports,* 1962, **10,** 483–486.

Suydam, M. M., & Myers, J. L. Some parameters of risk-taking behavior. *Psychological Reports,* 1962, **10,** 559–562.

14 B
EXPERIMENT
THE RISKY SHIFT:
HOW GROUP DISCUSSION
AFFECTS RISK TAKING

Decisions concerning risk taking may be strongly influenced by group discussion. Using paper-and-pencil questionnaires incorporating choice dilemmas similar to those found in everyday life, a number of studies (e.g., Wallach & Kogan, 1965; and Wallach, Kogan, & Bem, 1962) have shown that individuals changed their risk-taking levels toward greater levels of risk following a group discussion of the problem. The control subjects, who also took the test twice but without an intervening group discussion of the choice dilemmas, showed significantly less shift.

This effect, termed the risky shift, has been attributed to a variety of factors such as the diffusion of responsibility that exists when a group rather than an individual makes a decision. It has also been suggested that the group discussion allows social comparison processes to occur that induce more conservative members to shift their risk level toward greater risk. Clark and Willems (1969) have suggested that the risky shift is an artifact and slightly changing the wording of the instructions eliminates the risky shift. Critics such as Cartwright (1971, 1973) and Clark (1971) have raised serious questions about the value of research conducted in the area of the risky shift because of methodological and conceptual limitations.

Despite the controversy, the topic is of obvious importance and may serve as an extension study that contrasts with the approach to the study of risk examined in Experiment 14A. Other interesting alternative strategies include naturalistic settings such as those reported by McCaulay, Stitt, Woods, and Lipton (1973), and Malamuth and Feshbach, (1972).

REFERENCES

Cartwright, D. Risk taking by individuals and groups: An assessment of research employing choice dilemmas. *Journal of Personality and Social Psychology,* 1971, **20**, 361–378.

Cartwright, D. Determinants of scientific progress: The case of the risky shift. *American Psychologist,* 1973, **28**, 222—231.

Clark, R. D. Group-induced shift toward risk: A critical appraisal. *Psychological Bulletin,* 1971, **76**, 251—270.

Clark, R. D., & Willems, E. P. Where is the risky shift? Dependence on instructions. *Journal of Personality and Social Psychology,* 1969, **13**, 215—221.

McCauley, C., Stitt, C. L., Woods, K., & Lipton, D. Group shift to caution at the race track. *Journal of Experimental and Social Psychology,* 1973, **9**, 80—86.

Malamuth, N. M., & Feshbach, S. Risky shift in a naturalistic setting. *Journal of Personality,* 1972, **40**, 38—49.

Wallach, M. A., & Kogan, N. The roles of information, discussion, and consensus in group risk taking. *Journal of Experimental and Social Psychology,* 1965, **1**, 1—19.

Wallach, M. A., Kogan, N., & Bem, D. J. Group influence on individual risk-taking. *Journal of Abnormal and Social Psychology,* 1962, **65**, 75—86.

DATA SUMMARY ON RISK TAKING: PROPORTIONS OF RISKS TAKEN PER TRIAL BLOCK

	Small-Range Group								Large-Range Group							
	Trial Block								Trial Block							
	1–25		26–50		51–75		76–100		1–25		26–50		51–75		76–100	
Deck 1 Outcome:	+	−	+	−	+	−	+	−	+	−	+	−	+	−	+	−
S 1																
2																
3																
4																
5																
Sn																
M																
SD																

15 A
EXPERIMENT
INVERTED ALPHABET PRINTING AS A FUNCTION OF DISTRIBUTION OF PRACTICE

In general, activities involving some degree of coordination of our sensory and motor abilities are referred to as perceptual motor skills. As with most other skills, practice and training play an important part in their development and performance. One aspect of interest to psychologists has been the temporal conditions under which practice of such skills occur. The distribution of practice may either be massed (short or no intervening rest periods) or spaced (long intervening rest periods). It should be noted that massed and spaced are relative rather than absolute terms.

One perceptual motor task which has been frequently studied is inverted alphabet printing. The task of the subject is simply to print the letters of the alphabet in inverted form. Although the task is simple it is a convenient means for studying how distribution of practice affects the performance of motor skills. Archer (1954) and Kimble (1949b) have demonstrated that spaced practice leads to better performance than massed practice on this task.

One goal of these studies was to test some aspects of behavior theory as proposed by Hall (1943) but their theoretical significance need not concern us here. A brief account of the theoretical implications of the studies of the effects of the distribution of practice on motor learning can be found in Kimble (1949a). The present experiment will be concerned primarily with the assessment of the effects of three conditions of distribution of practice on performance of inverted alphabet printing.

METHOD

Subjects

Each experimenter will obtain three subjects of similar age. Assign one subject to each of the three distribution of practice conditions by some unbiased method.

Materials

Several sheets of lined notebook paper and a pencil will be required. A stop watch or a watch with a sweep second hand will also be needed.

Design

The experiment will compare three conditions that vary in the length of the intertrial interval (ITI). As in Archer's (1954) study, a trial will consist of 30 seconds during which the subject performs the task. Different groups will receive ITIs of differing duration. For one condition (Group 0), there will be no ITI; for another condition (Group 15) there will be a 15 second ITI between each trial, during which the subject is permitted to rest; for the third condition (Group 30) there will be a 30-second ITI between each trial, during which the subject is permitted to rest. The subjects in all conditions will receive a total of 20 trials.

Procedure

After seating your subject in a place free from distraction, give him several sheets of lined paper and a pencil and read the following instructions:

This experiment is a study of some aspects of how people perform skills involving motor coordination. During this session you will be asked to print in *alphabetical order* the letters of the alphabet in an *inverted* or upside-down arrangement.

You are to concentrate on speed primarily since your score depends on how many letters you print correctly. If you knowingly make a mistake, simply print right over it and continue printing. It might help you to know that certain letters are exactly the same whether printed upside down or rightside up, such as H, I, N, O, S, X, and Z. When I give you the signal, start printing from the right side to the left side of the paper starting on the top line of the paper and printing the alphabet upside down and in alphabetical order. When you complete one line, continue with the next line until you complete the page. Each time you complete the alphabet simply start printing the alphabet again from that point on the page. Continue in this manner until I ask you to stop.

For Group 0, the task requires 10 minutes of continuous practice (20 trials of 30 seconds each). In order to later measure the subject's performance on each trial, it will be necessary to ask the subject to "skip two lines" after each trial of 30 seconds. This method of distinguishing between trials should also be employed for Groups 15 and 30 to insure that conditions of practice be as similar as possible among the three conditions except for that of the intertrial interval.

Read the following additional instructions to Group 0:

So that I can evaluate your performance on this task after differing amounts of practice, I will ask you to *skip two lines* on your paper after every 30 seconds of practice. Then continue printing with the next letter of the alphabet after the last one you printed.

Read the following additional instructions to Group 15 and 30:

This command will occur at regular intervals. You will then sit quietly and rest for a short period. [Allow the subject to rest for the appropriate interval.]

When I tell you to resume printing, start with the next letter after the last one you printed. However, *skip two lines* before you resume printing so that I can evaluate your performance on this task after differing amounts of practice.

For Groups 15 and 30, say "Stop" at the end of each trial. Allow the subject to rest for the appropriate interval, then say "Skip two lines and resume printing." Continue in the appropriate manner described above for each condition until 20 trials have been completed.

Analysis of data

Determine for each of your subjects the total number of correct letters printed on each of the 20 trials. Combine the class data for each of the three conditions of practice to obtain the mean number of correct letters printed for each condition.

Plot a graph showing the performance curve for the combined data for each condition. Place the trials along the abscissa and the mean performance score along the ordinate.

Perform a one-way analysis of variance on the mean number of correct letters for the three conditions. If the overall F ratio is significant, compute individual t tests between the three conditions taken pairwise.

DISCUSSION

1. Compare your class findings with those of Archer (1954) and Kimble (1949b) which demonstrated superior performance with spaced practice. How do you account for the similarities or differences among the studies?

2. Do all conditions show improvement with practice? Is the rate of improvement visually different among the three conditions? (Note: The steeper the slope of the performance curve, the higher the rate of improvement.)

3. Assuming your class results show spaced practice to facilitate performance, what explanation can you offer?

4. Archer and Bourne (1956) distinguish between two processes which may be affected by spaced practice, namely, the actual time for printing each letter and the time for traveling from one letter to the next. Assuming your experiment shows facilitation or improved performance with spaced practice, which of the two processes mentioned by Archer and Bourne do you think was likely to have been affected?

5. What do you think would be the effect of longer ITIs on performance? Explain your rationale.

REFERENCES

Archer, E. J. Postrest performance in motor learning as a function of prerest degree of distribution of practice. *Journal of Experimental Psychology,* 1954, **47**, 47–51.

Archer, E. J., & Bourne, L. E., Jr. Inverted-alphabet printing as a function of intertrial rest and sex. *Journal of Experimental Psychology,* 1956, **52**, 322–328.

Hull, C. L. *Principles of behavior.* New York: Appleton-Century-Crofts, 1943.

Kimble, G. A. An experimental test of a two-factor theory of inhibition. *Journal of Experimental Psychology,* 1949, **39,** 15–23. (a)

Kimble, G. A. Performance and reminiscence in motor learning as a function of the degree of distribution of practice. *Journal of Experimental Psychology,* 1949, **39,** 500–510. (b)

15 B
EXPERIMENT
GENERALITY OF
THE BENEFITS OF
DISTRIBUTED PRACTICE

How does distributed practice affect performance on types of tasks where interference is involved? Another perceptual motor task involves the pursuit rotor which requires the subject to track a rotating target with a stylus. Digman (1959) has shown superior performance with distributed practice on this task also. It is generally assumed that distributed practice facilitates rote memory although Underwood (1961) has shown that the relationships cannot be described in simple terms. A useful extension to the study on distribution of practice might be to examine its effect on some other task involving interference.

One such task that apparently has not been examined in this respect is an intriguing phenomenon named after its founder, Stroop (1935). A list of color names such as red, green, blue, and so on are printed in a variety of colors other than the color names. On the Stroop test, the subject must name the colors (not the words) as fast as he can. Considerable interference occurs as is evidenced by the fact that subjects often read the words aloud rather than name the color in which the word is printed. An extensive review of research on the Stroop phenomenon was done by Dyer (1973) and no direct tests of the influence of distributed practice with this task were reported. Is the type of interference that occurs on this task similar to that encountered on the inverted alphabet printing task where old habits must be suppressed in order to perform the required responses? A comparison of massed and distributed practice on the Stroop test should give some suggestive evidence.

REFERENCES

Digman, J. M. Growth of a motor skill as a function of distribution of practice. *Journal of Experimental Psychology,* 1959, **57**, 310–316.

Dyer, F. N. The Stroop phenomenon and its use in the study of perceptual, cognitive, and response processes. *Memory and Cognition,* 1973, **1,** 106–120.

Stroop, J. R. Studies of interference in serial reactions. *Journal of Experimental Psychology,* 1935, **18,** 643–662.

Underwood, B. J. Ten years of massed practice on distributed practice. *Psychological Review,* 1961, **68,** 229–247.

DATA SUMMARY ON INVERTED ALPHABET PRINTING: NUMBER OF PRINTED LETTERS PER TRIAL

	\multicolumn{21}{c}{Group 0}
	\multicolumn{21}{c}{Trial}
	1	2	3	4	5	6	7	8	9	10	11	12	13	14	15	16	17	18	19	20	Σ
S																					
1																					
2																					
3																					
4																					
5																					
Sn																					

M   M

SD

DATA SUMMARY ON INVERTED ALPHABET PRINTING: NUMBER OF PRINTED LETTERS PER TRIAL

	Group 15																				
	Trial																				
	1	2	3	4	5	6	7	8	9	10	11	12	13	14	15	16	17	18	19	20	Σ
S																					
1																					
2																					
3																					
4																					
5																					
Sn																					

M   M

SD

DATA SUMMARY ON INVERTED ALPHABET PRINTING: NUMBER OF PRINTED LETTERS PER TRIAL

	1	2	3	4	5	6	7	8	9	10	11	12	13	14	15	16	17	18	19	20	Σ
S																					
1																					
2																					
3																					
4																					
5																					
Sn																					

Group 30

Trial

M   M

SD

16 A
EXPERIMENT
ORDER EFFECTS IN PERSONALITY IMPRESSION FORMATION

How do we form our impressions about the personalities of people we meet? Personality refers to a combination of traits inferred from samples of observed behavior of the person in question. Although the observations we make of a person on our initial encounter do not permit an accurate or complete determination of his personality, nonetheless it is evident that we are continually forming impressions of personality on the basis of limited contact with other people, regardless of the accuracy of such judgments.

There may be considerable truth to the adage "first impressions are lasting ones." In any case, we do tend to classify and judge personality from limited initial impressions. Some experimental evidence to support this assertion comes from Asch (1946). He had subjects report impressions of a hypothetical person who was described by the experimenter using a list of adjectives allegedly applicable to the fictitious person to be judged. This list included both favorable and unfavorable adjectives applicable to the fictitious person; however, the order in which the list of adjectives was presented differed for the two groups. In one group the favorable adjectives were read first, followed by the unfavorable ones, whereas in the other group the opposite order was used.

Asch found that the impressions formed were related to the type of adjectives read first, that is, the same list evoked favorable impressions in the group receiving favorable adjectives first, whereas it evoked unfavorable impressions in the group receiving unfavorable adjectives first. Apparently, then, *primacy* is an important factor in impression formation.

Such primary effects in impression formation from a list of adjectives have also been found by Anderson (1965). However, there is less agreement regarding the underlying causes for such primacy effects. Asch hypothesized that the meanings of later adjectives on the list are actually modified by the context set up by the initial adjectives presented

to the subject. Thus, if favorable adjectives are received first, they make the following unfavorable words seem less unfavorable. On the other hand, if unfavorable adjectives are presented first, they affect the subsequent favorable adjectives adversely with the result that they appear less favorable.

Anderson and Hubert (1963), on the other hand, found evidence to support an alternative explanation, namely, that the subject simply pays less attention to later adjectives on the list, and therefore they do not have as much influence on the impression formed as the early adjectives on the list. It is important to note that although this explanation differs from Asch's, both experimenters agree in their results, that is, that primacy effects occur.

This experiment combines aspects of both the Asch study and the Anderson and Hubert experiment and provides for an examination of order effects on impression formation using the Asch procedure of presenting adjectives describing a hypothetical person.

METHOD

Subjects

Each experimenter should obtain four subjects, two for each order of the list. Devise some unbiased method of assigning subjects to the two conditions.

Materials

The list of adjectives describing a hypothetical person is provided in Table 16.1 in the two different orders used by Asch. Table 16.3 contains an adjective check list, which the subject will complete after he has formed his impression.

Procedure

After seating your subject in a quiet room, read the following instructions:

I am interested in your impression of a person you do not know but whom I will describe to you by reading a list of adjectives which were given by some of this person's acquaintances when they were asked to describe this person. Listen carefully since I

TABLE 16.1:   TWO DIFFERENT ORDERS OF ADJECTIVES DESCRIBING UNKNOWN PERSON*

Order FU (Favorable-Unfavorable)	*Order UF (Unfavorable-Favorable)*
Intelligent	Envious
Industrious	Stubborn
Impulsive	Critical
Critical	Impulsive
Stubborn	Industrious
Envious	Intelligent

*Adapted from Asch, 1946.

cannot repeat any of the list. Later, I will ask you for your impression of this person.

Read the list of adjectives in Table 16.1 about the rate of one every 3 seconds. Use order FU for your first and fourth subjects and order UF for your second and third subjects. After you have completed the list, provide the subject with paper and ask him to write a short paragraph describing his personal impression of this unknown person. Instruct the subject that he may have as much time as he wishes.

Then take the descriptive paragraph away from the subject and read the following instructions to him:

I want you to choose a number from 1 (Very unfavorable) to 9 (Very favorable) which reflects how you would rate your impression of this person.

Place the rating scale in Table 16.2 before the subject to assist him in making his rating.

When he has completed his task, give him the adjective check list provided in Table 16.3 and read the following instruction to the subject.

Check off only those adjectives, if any, which you think are applicable to this person.

TABLE 16.2: RATING SCALE

Very unfavorable ⊢⊣ 1 2 3 4 5 6 7 8 9 Very favorable

TABLE 16.3:   ADJECTIVE CHECK LIST*

Generous	Humane
Wise	Good-looking
Happy	Persistent
Good-natured	Serious
Humorous	Restrained
Sociable	Altruistic
Popular	Imaginative
Reliable	Strong
Important	Honest

*Adapted from Asch, 1946.

Analysis of data

When the class meets, a few experimenters should read the descriptive paragraph written by one of their subjects. This will give the entire class an idea of the range of impressions formed by their subjects. *At no time, however, should the experimenter disclose to the class what order of the list his subject received.*

Each description collected by the experimenters will be read without announcing to which group the subject who wrote the passage was assigned, and all class members (experimenters) will rate the description from 1 (Very unfavorable) to 9 (Very favorable). After *all* descriptions have been rated separately by the experimenters, the class *average rating* for each description will be computed. Then a comparison will be made of the mean favorableness-unfavorableness of the blind ratings by all experimenters of the descriptions written by the subjects in the FU and the UF groups, using a *t* test for uncorrelated data.

The adjective check list data will be analyzed by determining the mean number of times each adjective was checked by subjects in the two groups. Try to make a visual inspection of the relative usages of the different adjectives in the check list to see if they differed for the two list orders. Compare visually the number of times each adjective was used by subjects in the two groups.

Next determine the mean ratings of the hypothetical person given by the subjects of each group. Check to see which group gives the higher mean rating toward favorableness. If Group FU gives a significantly higher mean rating toward favorableness than Group UF, this would indicate that primary effects were present. If Group UF gives a significantly higher mean rating toward favorableness than Group FU, this would suggest that recency effects were more potent than primacy effects.

DISCUSSION

1. Considering each of the three major dependent variables separately, i.e., experimenters' ratings of descriptive paragraphs, subjects' adjective check lists, and subjects' ratings of favorableness-unfavorableness, discuss the evidence for or against primacy as a factor in impression formation. Are there any discrepancies among the outcomes from the three measures which would lead to contradictory conclusions regarding primacy?

2. What arguments can you offer for or against the use of any of the three response measures as an index of the impression formed?

3. What advantages and disadvantages can you see in the Asch technique of assessing impression formation? What other techniques can you suggest for studying impression formation?

4. The sequence of the three adjectives *within* each category, F and U, differ in the two orders, FU and UF. What effect, if any, would this fact have on the results?

5. What changes do you think are needed in the Adjective Check List, Table 16.3? How would these modifications constitute improvements?

6. In this experiment, each subject was tested on all three measures in the same sequence. Suggest an alternative design and compare it with the present design.

REFERENCES

Anderson, N. H. Primacy effects in personality formation using a generalized order effect paradigm. *Journal of Personality and Social Psychology,* 1965, **2,** 1—9.

Anderson, N. H., & Hubert, S. Effects of concomitant verbal recall on order effects in personality impression formation. *Journal of Verbal Learning and Verbal Behavior,* 1963, **2,** 379—391.

Asch, S. E. Forming impressions of personality. *Journal of Abnormal and Social Psychology,* 1946, **41,** 258–290.

SELECTED BIBLIOGRAPHY

Anderson, N. H. Likeableness ratings of 555 personality-trait words. *Journal of Personality and Social Psychology,* 1968, **9,** 272–279.

Anderson, N. H., & Barrios, A. A. Primacy effects in personality impression formation. *Journal of Abnormal and Social Psychology,* 1961, **63,** 346–350.

Anderson, N. H. & Jacobson, A. Effect of stimulus inconsistency and discounting instructions in personality impression formation. *Journal of Personality and Social Psychology.* 1965, **2,** 531–539.

Anderson, N. H., & Norman, A. Order effects in impression formation on four classes of stimuli. *Journal of Abnormal and Social Psychology,* 1964, **69,** 467–471.

Kelley, H. H. The warm-cold variables in first impressions of persons. *Journal of Personality,* 1950, **18,** 431–439.

Loewenthal, K. How are first impressions formed. *Psychological Reports,* 1967, **21,** 834–836.

Wischner, J. Reanalysis of "Impressions of Personality." *Psychological Review,* 1960, **67,** 96–112.

Wyer, R. S., & Watson, S. F. Context effects in impression formation. *Journal of Personality and Social Psychology,* 1969, **12,** 22–23.

16 B
EXPERIMENT
ORDER EFFECTS IN
ATTRIBUTION OF ABILITY

The influence of order of information is not limited to impressions of personality and should be manifest in a variety of other types of judgments. For example, judgments of the ability of others may be influenced by the order in which we receive information about their performance in a given situation. How would a professor's opinion of a student whose examination scores improved from C to B to A over successive tests differ from that formed of a student whose scores deteriorated from A to B to C on the same tests? Even though the total points achieved might be the same, would the patterns of performance lead to different impressions? If so, would there be a primacy or recency effect in terms of which performance was given greater weight?

Jones, Rock, Shaver, Goethals, and Ward (1968) provided some evidence pertaining to these questions. Subjects watched confederates of the experimenter solve 30 problems similar to those on intellectual aptitude tests. Confederates always solved only 15 problems but some showed gradual improvement while others showed gradual deterioration of performance. Jones et al. found a tendency for subjects to show a primacy effect, judging persons who showed good initial but poor later performance as more intelligent and capable. Perhaps the subjects discounted the poor scores on the latter part of the test by attributing them to boredom, fatigue, etc. In any case, primacy on first impressions appeared to affect observers' attributions of ability.

A worthwhile extension of Experiment 16A might be to replicate the Jones et al. (1968) study to examine the generalizability of primacy.

REFERENCE

Jones, E. E., Rock, L., Shaver, K. G., Goethals, G. R., & Ward, L. M. Pattern of performance and ability attribution: An unexpected primary effect. *Journal of Personality and Social Psychology*, 1968, **10**, 317–340.

17 A
EXPERIMENT
THE EFFECTS OF
ANXIETY ON TALKING

Anxiety is a condition of considerable interest to psychologists, particularly clinicians, since it is often disruptive in its effects on behavior (Young, 1949). On the other hand, mild levels of anxiety can sometimes improve the quality of performance (Leeper, 1948). In order to account for these apparently contradictory effects, psychologists have proposed that there may be a nonmonotonic or inverted U function between arousal dimensions such as anxiety and performance (Hebb, 1955). In other words, performance may be poor with low anxiety, increase to some optimal level with moderate anxiety or stress, and then deteriorate with high levels of anxiety.

One interesting situation in which one could study the effects of anxiety is public speaking. We are all familiar, directly or indirectly, with the anxiety known commonly as "stagefright" or audience anxiety. Perfectly calm and rational persons suddenly go to pieces, stammer and stutter, argue illogically, and tremble when called on to talk before an audience. A review of studies on talking behavior before audiences by Murray (1971), indicated that a number of factors such as the size of the audience, the reaction of the audience, and the topic to be presented can affect anxiety.

Levin, Baldwin, Gallwey, and Paivio (1960), for example, used children of age 10—12 years who were to present their own short stories before either the experimenter or an audience of seven adults. It was assumed that the larger audience involved more stress. Significantly shorter stories were given before the larger audience.

In the present study we will compare the effects of three different sizes of audience, 1, 3, and 7 persons, on the performance of subjects instructed to talk about a given topic. Measures will be made of the length of the talk as well as the frequency of silent pauses exceeding 5 seconds, and the ratio of the number of such pauses per minute of speaking.

According to the inverted U hypothesis, performance should be optimal with an intermediate-sized audience. Longer and clearer talks with fewer pauses should occur. However, it is conceivable that stress and anxiety may be so high even with an audience of one that no differences will be obtained or that the best performance will occur with an audience of only about one person rather than with an audience of three.

METHOD

Subjects

Obtain three subjects, one for each test condition. Assign your subjects to the conditions in some unbiased manner.

Materials

A stop watch or a watch with a sweep second hand will be needed for timing duration of talk and silent pauses.

Procedure

It may be convenient for several students to work in teams so as to create the 3- and 7-person audience conditions. As an alternative, you could obtain friends to assist you by serving as your audience in those two conditions. Include yourself as one member of the audience in all three conditions. Instruct your assistants to act naturally, merely to listen and not talk with your subject, you, or each other in order that the speaker will not be disrupted.

Read the following instructions to each subject:

We are interested in studying aspects of extemporaneous or impromptu speeches and want you to make a speech off the top of your head. Your topic will be: *The pros and cons of the women's liberation movement*. You may have 5 minutes to collect your thoughts and ideas. You will be asked to speak for about 5 minutes or as long as you find it necessary to express your views. While you speak, I will be making notes about your speech, but try to ignore me. Do you have any questions? All right, I will come for you in about 5 minutes to begin your speech.

Seat your subject in a quiet place, free from distractions, for 5 minutes and then summon him into the room where the speech is to be given. When you are ready give him a signal to begin. If your subject cannot speak for a full 5 minutes, allow him to stop whenever he wishes. The purpose of the instruction to speak for about 5 minutes is to encourage speeches that are long enough to provide adequate data.

Record the total time between the beginning signal and the end of the talk. Place a tally mark on your data sheet for each silent pause exceeding 5 seconds. Members of your audience are present merely to serve as a source of anxiety for your subject. However, their comments may be helpful later in analyzing your data.

Analysis of data

Combine your results with those of the rest of the class. Determine the mean duration of the talks, the mean number of silent pauses, and the mean ratio of the number of pauses to the duration for each audience size. Calculate a one-way analysis of variance of each of these dependent variables.

DISCUSSION

1. What effect did audience size have on each dependent variable? Do these findings support the inverted U hypothesis? If not, can you offer an explanation for the discrepancy? How can you test your answer?

2. Did you notice any substantial individual differences in response to the presence of an audience? Are some people more anxiety-prone and others anxiety-resistant?

3. Do you think the type of topic might influence the results? If so, what type of topic would increase the effect and which type would reduce the effect of anxiety? Why?

4. Do you think audience size might have affected such aspects of speech as clarity and persuasiveness? How would you determine the presence of such an effect?

REFERENCES

Hebb, D. O. Drives and the C. N. S. (conceptual nervous system). *Psychological Review,* 1955, **62,** 243–254.

Leeper, R. W. A motivational theory of emotion to replace "Emotion as a disorganized response." *Psychological Review,* 1948, **55,** 5–21.

Levin, H., Baldwin, A. L., Gallwey, M., & Paivio, A. Audience stress, personality, and speech. *Journal of Abnormal and Social Psychology,* 1960, **61,** 469–473.

Murray, D. C. Talk, silence, and anxiety. *Psychological Bulletin,* 1971, **75,** 244–260.

Young, P. T. Emotion as disorganized response: A reply to Professor Leeper. *Psychological Review,* 1949, **56,** 184–191.

SELECTED BIBLIOGRAPHY

Droppleman, L. F., & McNair, D. M. An experimental analog of public speaking. *Journal of Consulting and Clinical Psychology,* 1971, **36,** 91–96.

Lipper, S., & McNair, D. M. Simulated public speaking and anxiety. *Journal of Experimental Research in Personality,* 1972, **6,** 237–240.

17 B
EXPERIMENT
A COMPARISON
OF STATE AND TRAIT
ANXIETY ON TALKING

Anxiety is not only a function of the situation but may also differ from individual to individual. In other words, some persons are generally more anxious than other persons over a variety of situations. Psychologists such as Spielberger, Gorsuch, and Lushene (1970) refer to anxiety both as a relatively permanent *trait* and as a temporary *state*.

In summarizing the results of studies relating trait anxiety and talk, Murray (1971) found a positive correlation such that the higher the trait anxiety, the more the verbal output. On the other hand, the relationship between situational or state anxiety and verbal performance showed a nonmonotonic or inverted U function. Thus, more verbal output occurred with state anxiety up to some point after which it reversed and began to decrease. Murray concluded that some of the disagreement among studies may be due to the failure to study both types of anxiety. For example, studies of trait anxiety do not usually vary state anxiety (Preston & Gardner, 1967) while studies of state anxiety do not often vary trait anxiety (Levin, Baldwin, Gallwey, Paivio, 1960).

An interesting extension study might be to examine the influence of both types of anxiety. Persons varying in trait anxiety might be identified by use of a general anxiety scale (Spielberger, Gorsuch, & Lushene, 1970; Taylor, 1953) or with a scale developed especially to measure speech anxiety (Lamb, 1972). Half of the subjects at each level of trait anxiety could then be tested under low and half under high situational or state anxiety conditions.

REFERENCES

Lamb, D. H. Speech anxiety: Towards a theoretical conceptualization and preliminary scale development. *Speech Monographs,* 1972, **39,** 62–67.

Levin, H., Baldwin, A. L., Gallwey, M., & Paivio, A. Audience stress, personality, and speech. *Journal of Abnormal and Social Psychology,* 1960, **61,** 469–473.

Murray, D. C. Talk, silence, and anxiety. *Psychological Bulletin,* 1971, **75,** 244–266.

Preston, J. M., & Gardner, R. C. Dimensions of oral and written language fluency. *Journal of Verbal Learning and Verbal Behavior,* 1967, **6,** 936–945.

Spielberger, C. D., Gorsuch, R., & Lushene, R. *STAI Manual for the State Trait Anxiety Inventory.* Palo Alto: Consulting Psychologists Press, 1970.

Taylor, J. A. A personality scale of manifest anxiety. *Journal of Abnormal and Social Psychology,* 1953, **48,** 285–290.

DATA SUMMARY ON TALK AND ANXIETY AUDIENCE SIZE

Audience Size																	
7	Ratio No./Minute																M SD
	Number of Pauses																M SD
	Duration																M SD
		S_1	2	3	4	5										S_n	
3	Ratio No./Minute																M SD
	Number of Pauses																M SD
	Duration																M SD
		S_1	2	3	4	5										S_n	
1	Ratio No./Minute																M SD
	Number of Pauses																M SD
	Duration																M SD
		S_1	2	3	4	5										S_n	

18 A
EXPERIMENT
REACTIONS TO INVASION
OF PERSONAL SPACE

It has been observed among various species that there is a tendency for organisms to stake out territory that is defended if it is invaded. The territorial imperative, as Ardrey (1966) termed it, has been compared to similar behavior in humans by anthropologists (e.g., Hall, 1966) and psychologists (e.g., Sommer, 1969). It appears that humans prefer a certain amount of personal space and if it is threatened, there is an attempt to defend it or to flee from it. Even though cultural factors affect the exact nature and extent of personal space, the evidence suggests that the tendency to react to invasions of one's personal space elicits some type of defense or flight in all societies.

Sommer (1969) and his associates have performed a number of field studies (e.g., Felipe & Sommer, 1966; Sommer & Becker, 1969) in which they attempted to assess factors that influence defense of personal space. The present study is an attempt to replicate some of their work that they conducted in natural surroundings, such as university libraries. Felipe and Sommer (1966) observed the reactions of female students seated alone at reading tables when a female confederate of the experimenter invaded the table and sat down. In comparison to control subjects (female students whose personal space was not invaded), there was a significantly greater proportion of girls who left their tables within the 30 minute observation period following the invasion. This flight response was interpreted as stemming from the threat that the invasion represented. It was also noted that before the flight occurred, the target persons engaged in various behaviors that could be considered defensive, such as arranging books and supplies to set up barriers or placing coats on adjacent chairs to "reserve" them.

METHOD

Subjects

Each pair of student experimenters should test four female subjects, two in the experimental and two in the control conditions.

Materials

No special materials will be needed other than notebooks and textbooks for the invader to use in the library.

Procedure

Students should work in teams of one male and one female experimenter. The female experimenter will "invade" the personal space of the first and third female student found in the library seated alone at a rectangular reading table which can seat at least six and no more than eight students. The female experimenter should take the seat directly opposite the target person. The second and fourth female student seated alone at the same type of table and in the same relative seat at the table will serve as control subjects and will not have the personal space invaded. The male experimenter will make observations from a vantage point several tables away from which he can get a frontal view of the target person and her behavior. He should take care to be unobtrusive so that his observation is not noticed by the target person since that might influence her to leave.

In order to minimize the chances that target persons will leave for classes before the experiment can be completed, limit the start of your invasions to the period of about 5 to 10 minutes after classes usually start. Similarly, to avoid the chance that other persons will invade the personal space of the target person, try to conduct your observations during hours when the library is uncrowded. Otherwise, you will lose subjects if other persons come and sit at the table that you are observing.

The invasion should last 15 minutes or until the target person leaves, and does not return, whichever comes sooner. The invader should take three books, sit down and study, and not engage in any conversation with the target person. The observer should note the target person's reaction to the invasion, for example, smiling or frowning at the invader, postural changes, leaving the table, and so on, as well as time of departure if the target person leaves.

Analysis of data

Combine the class data and compare the proportions of experimental and control subjects who leave and do not return during the 15-minute test period. Test for the significance of the difference between the proportions using z for a difference between uncorrelated proportions (Guilford, 1965, p. 186). You can also compute mean time to departure for the two groups and compare the means using a t test for independent data.

DISCUSSION

1. Did your observations of the target persons show fidgeting, looking at the invader, and so on, that might suggest any annoyance at the invasion? Could these observations be affected by experimenter bias? If so, how would you control against bias?

2. What difference would it make if the invader had been male? Do you think male targets would react in the same way as female targets did to female invaders? To male invaders? That is, do you think results would vary as a function of the sex of the invaders? Sex of the target? Explain.

3. The type of invasion can vary in the situation that you have studied. What difference do you think it would have made if instead of sitting directly opposite the target, the invader sat alongside the target but one seat away? Why?

4. The intervention of naturally occurring behavior was minimal in this experiment. However, there are many other field experiments with more dramatic events, such as staged liquor store robberies (Darley & Latane', 1970) fake passing out in public places (Piliavin, Rodin, & Piliavin, 1969), or contrived roadside flat tires (Bryan & Test, 1967). What ethical problems, if any, do you see in this type of naturalistic research?

REFERENCES

Ardrey, R. *The territorial imperative.* New York: Atheneum, 1966.

Bryan, J. H., & Test, M. A. Models and helping: Naturalistic studies of aiding behavior. *Journal of Personality and Social Psychology,* 1967, **6**, 400–407.

Darley, J., & Latané, B. *The unresponsive bystander: Why doesn't he help?* New York: Appleton-Century, 1970.

Felipe, N., & Sommer, R. Invasions of personal space. *Social Problems,* 1966, **14**, 206–214.

Guilford, J. P. *Fundamental statistics in psychology and education.* (4th ed.) New York: McGraw-Hill, 1965.

Hall, E. T. *The hidden dimension.* Garden City: Doubleday, 1966.

Piliavin, I. M., Rodin, J., & Piliavin, J. A. Good samaritanism: An underground phenomenon? *Journal of Personality and Social Psychology,* 1969, **13**, 289–299.

Sommer, R. *Personal space, the behavioral basis of design.* Englewood Cliffs, N. J.: Prentice-Hall, 1969.

Sommer, R., & Becker, F. D. Territorial defense and the good neighbor. *Journal of Personality and Social Psychology,* 1969, **11**, 85–92.

SELECTED BIBLIOGRAPHY

Ellsworth, P. C., Carlsmith, J. M., & Henson, A. The stare as a stimulus to flight in human subjects. *Journal of Personality and Social Psychology,* 1972, **21**, 302–311.

Evans, G. W., & Howard, R. B. Personal space. *Psychological Bulletin,* 1973, **80**, 334–344.

Sommer, R. Small group ecology. *Psychological Bulletin,* 1967, **67,** 145–152.

18 B
EXPERIMENT
DEFENSE OF PERSONAL
SPACE BY NEIGHBORS

Sommer and Becker (1969) conducted a series of related studies directed at investigating factors which might affect the extent to which a neighbor might defend territory from invasion for an absent neighbor.

In one study, a neighbor relationship was established by having a confederate of the experimenter assume a seat on the same side of an otherwise empty library table as the subject. One seat in between the two was left vacant. After either 5 minutes or 20 minutes, the confederate left his books on the table to serve as markers for his space and departed. Then a second confederate invaded the space either 15 minutes or 60 minutes later and asked the subject whether or not the vacated seat was taken.

The neighbor was more likely to "defend" the vacated seat if the invasion was made shortly after the first confederate departed than after the longer interval. The amount of time which the first confederate occupied the seat, 5 minutes or 20 minutes, before leaving made no difference.

An extension of the personal space study might be based on the Summer and Becker study of the behavior of the neighbor.

REFERENCES

Sommer, R., & Becker, F. D. Territorial defense and the good neighbor. *Journal of Personality and Social Psychology,* 1969, **11,** 85–92.

DATA SUMMARY ON PERSONAL SPACE INVASION: REACTIONS OF TARGETS (LV=LEAVE: ST=STAY)

Time to Departure

	Experimental Group			Control Group	Observations/Notes
S 1		S 1			
2		2			
3		3			
4		4			
S_n		S_n			
M		M			
SD		SD			

KEY TO SELECTED TEXTBOOKS

The set of experiments in this manual is well-suited for use in conjunction with a number of textbooks commonly used in courses in experimental method and design in psychology. Some of these texts place more emphasis on research designs and procedures while others also devote attention to specific content areas. Therefore, the key has been constructed to coordinate this manual with chapters in some of the texts on the basis of research design and with chapters in other texts on the basis of content.

Jung & Bailey Experiments	Major Research Designs	Matheson, Bruce & Beauchamp (1974)	McGuigan (1968)	Underwood & Shaughnessey (1975)	Wood (1974)
5A, 8A, 12A, 13A, 16A, 18A	1. Randomized Groups (Independent Groups) A. 1 Independent Variable 2 groups	Ch. 4	Ch. 5	Ch. 3	Ch. 5, 7, 9, 10
7A, 10A, 15A, 17A	B. 1 Independent Variable More than 2 groups	Ch. 5	Ch. 9	Ch. 3	Ch. 5, 7, 9, 10
1A, 3A, 4A, 9A	C. 2 Independent Variables (Factorial Design)	Ch. 5	Ch. 10	Ch. 5	Ch. 5, 7, 9, 10
14A 2A, 3A, 6A, 11A	2. Within Groups and Counterbalancing	Ch. 4,5 Ch. 3	Ch. 11 Ch. 6	Ch. 4	Ch. 6, 7, 11

Jung & Bailey Experiments	Major Content Topics	Andreas (1972)	Calfee (1975)	Underwood (1966)
1AB, 2AB, 3AB, 7AB	1. Problems of Method and Design (e.g., experimenter bias, demand characteristics)	Ch. 2, 3	Ch. 3	Ch. 7, 11
6AB, 7AB, 8AB, 9AB, 10AB	2. Learning and Memory	Ch. 9, 11	Ch. 9, 16, 19	Ch. 11, 12
4AB, 15AB	3. Perception and Motor Skills	Ch. 5, 10	Ch. 6, 8, 12, 13	Ch. 6, 8
5AB, 7AB, 12AB, 13AB, 16AB	4. Cognition and Problem Solving	Ch. 13	Ch. 15, 21	Ch. 10, 13
11AB, 14AB, 17AB	5. Motivation and Emotion	Ch. 14		
3B, 14B 16AB, 17B, 18AB	6. Social and Personality	Ch. 15		

REFERENCES

Andreas, B. G. *Experimental psychology.* (2nd ed.) New York: Wiley, 1972.

Calfee, R. C. *Human experimental psychology.* New York: Holt, Rinehart and Winston, 1975.

Matheson, D. W., Bruce, R. L., & Beauchamp, K. L. *Introduction to experimental psychology.* (2nd ed.) New York: Holt, Rinehart and Winston, 1974.

McGuigan, F. J. *Experimental psychology: A methodological approach.* (2nd ed.) Englewood Cliffs, N. J.: Prentice-Hall, 1968.

Underwood, B. J. *Experimental psychology.* (2nd ed.) New York: Appleton, 1966.

Underwood, B. J., & Shaughnessey, J. J. *Experimentation in psychology.* New York: Wiley, 1975.

Wood, G. *Fundamentals of psychological research.* Boston: Little, Brown and Co., 1974.